Whose Tale Is True?

Readers Theatre to Introduce and Research 49
Amazing American Women

Nancy Polette

Teacher Ideas Press

An imprint of Libraries Unlimited
Westport, Connecticut • London

Library of Congress Cataloging-in-Publication Data

Polette, Nancy.
  Whoses tale is true? : readers theatre to introduce and research 49 amazing American women / Nancy Polette.
     p. cm.
  Includes bibliographical references and index.
  ISBN 978-1-59158-762-0 (alk. paper)
  1. Biography—Study and teaching. 2. Women—United States—Biography. I. Title.
CT85.P65   2009
920.72—dc22   2008024063

British Library Cataloguing in Publication Data is available.

Library of Congress Catalog Card Number: 2008024063
ISBN: 978-1-59158-762-0

First published in 2009

Libraries Unlimited, 88 Post Road West, Westport, CT 06881
A Member of the Greenwood Publishing Group, Inc.
www.lu.com

Printed in the United States of America

The paper used in this book complies with the
Permanent Paper Standard issued by the National
Information Standards Organization (Z39.48–1984).

10 9 8 7 6 5 4 3 2 1

Contents

Introduction

Meet 49 amazing women who have used their talents to make unique contributions to American life. From political activists to scientists to opera divas, each woman has taken her passion and her gifts and developed them to the fullest. In doing so, each has found her place in history.

Each woman is introduced with a short play in which four students take roles: a host or hostess and three women all claiming to be the same person. Through *critical listening*, the audience will be able to identify which of the three is telling the truth. The pretenders either include a historical fact in their speeches that could not possibly be true or contradict themselves in a later speech. Each script is followed by a short reader response or research activity.

The performance format is ideal for all readers. The struggling reader is not overwhelmed by a full page of print he or she must decipher. Instead, the reader reads her part and then can prepare for the next speech while others are reading their parts. The competent reader benefits from the performance format by realizing the importance of slowing down and reading with expression. Many competent readers use the machine-gun approach to oral reading, falsely believing that rapid reading is desirable.

Finally, each short play can be used as a model for researching and reporting on the life of another famous person. An outline is provided for this purpose (see page 161). Students truly show understanding of the written word when they are able to encode it in a new form. The models in *Whose Tale Is True* allow them to do this and to create a finished product in which they can take pride.

Part One

Eighteenth Century

Deborah Sampson (1760–1827)

On the Front Lines in the Revolution

Reading Parts: Host, Deborah Sampson No. 1, Deborah Sampson No. 2, Deborah Sampson No. 3

Host: [facing audience] Welcome to "Whose Tale Is True?" Each of our three guests claims to be Deborah Sampson, combat soldier in the Revolutionary War. Only one, however, is telling the complete truth. It is up to you to decide which one is the real Deborah Sampson. Now let's meet our guests. [facing readers] Welcome. I understand that you were the first woman in the history of the nation to take part in combat. Can you tell us how that came about?

Deborah Sampson No. 1: I learned to be independent at an early age. I was the oldest of six children. My father abandoned us, and we lived in poverty. My mother could not work because of poor health, so it was up to me to look after my brothers and sisters. I really became the "man" of the family.

Deborah Sampson No. 2: I was born in 1760. When I was 10 years old my father abandoned the family, and I was sent to be an indentured servant in the household of Jeremiah Thomas. For 10 years I worked hard both in the house and in the fields. If anything would prepare someone for combat, that would!

Deborah Sampson No. 3: My life as an indentured servant was hard, but in the winter when there was less work I was allowed to attend school. I learned enough so that when the 10 years of my servitude were over I became a teacher.

Host: How did you go from teaching school to joining George Washington's army?

Deborah Sampson No. 1: I tired of teaching school and believed so fervently in freedom for the colonies that I put on blue jeans and a man's shirt, cut my hair, and enlisted in the Continental Army under the name Robert Shurtleff. I performed my duties as well as many men.

From *Whose Tale Is True?: Readers Theatre to Introduce and Research 49 Amazing American Women* by Nancy Polette. Westport, CT: Teacher Ideas Press. Copyright © 2008.

Deborah Sampson No. 2: Ten years of hard work as an indentured servant had made me as strong as most men. Also, at five feet seven inches I was tall for a woman. Back home some people guessed that I had enlisted in the army, and I was banned from the church for life.

Deborah Sampson No. 3: Other soldiers teased me abut not having to shave, but they thought I was just too young. In a battle at Tarrytown, New York, I was shot in the leg but did not dare ask for medical help. I tended the wound myself. I was not a very good doctor, and the wound healed badly. I limp to this day.

Host: Was your disguise as a man ever discovered?

Deborah Sampson No. 1: In 1783 I came down with a terrible fever. I was so delirious that I did not realize I was being taken to a hospital.

Deborah Sampson No. 2: The doctor who treated me discovered my secret, but he was very kind and made arrangements that allowed me to receive an honorable discharge from the army.

Deborah Sampson No. 3: I was discharged from the army in October 1783 and returned home to marry Benjamin Gannett. I went back to teaching school, although the old bullet wound in my arm continued to bother me. Paul Revere sent a letter to Congress about my service, and like the other soldiers I received a pension of four dollars a month. It was a large sum at that time. I have no regrets about my time as a soldier. I fought for freedom and would have it no other way.

Host: Now it is time to decide whose tale is true. We will vote by a show of hands. Is it No. 1? Is it No. 2? Is it No. 3? Now for the moment you have all been waiting for:

Will the real Deborah Sampson step forward?

Answer: No. 2

No. 1 mentioned blue jeans, which were not around in the 1700s.

No. 3 contradicted herself. The bullet wound was in her leg, not her arm.

FURTHER READING

McGovern, Ann. *Secret Soldier: The Story of Deborah Sampson.* Four Winds, 1975.

From *Whose Tale Is True?: Readers Theatre to Introduce and Research 49 Amazing American Women* by Nancy Polette. Westport, CT: Teacher Ideas Press. Copyright © 2008.

REPORTING ON DEBORAH SAMPSON

Compose an acrostic poem about Deborah Sampson. Each line begins with a letter of her name. The first line is done for you.

D eborah learned to be independent at an early age.

E _____

B _____

O _____

R _____

A _____

H _____

S _____

A _____

M _____

P _____

S _____

O _____

N _____

Mary Hays McCauly (Molly Pitcher) (1754–1832)

Sergeant Molly

Reading Parts: Host, Molly Pitcher No. 1, Molly Pitcher No. 2, Molly Pitcher No. 3

Host: [facing audience] Welcome to "Whose Tale Is True?" Each of our three guests claims to be Molly Pitcher, heroine of the American Revolution. Only one, however, is telling the complete truth. It is up to you to decide which one is the real Molly Pitcher. Now let's meet our guests. [facing readers] Welcome. I understand that as an artillery wife you traveled with your husband to war. Is that correct?

Molly Pitcher No. 1: That is correct. I grew up in the small town of Carlisle, Pennsylvania, and worked as a servant until my marriage at age 16. When my husband, William Hays, went to fight in the Revolutionary War, I went with him.

Molly Pitcher No. 2: It was the custom at that time for wives to accompany their husbands to war. We cooked for them and took care of their clothing. I even learned to clean William's Colt six shooter.

Molly Pitcher No. 3: When William and I were married, I thought we would have a quiet life in a sleepy little town. William made a good living as a barber, and we were very happy. Then the war came and William enlisted. I could do no less than accompany him.

Host: What was life on the battlefields like?

Molly Pitcher No. 1: It was terrible. If the heat didn't get you, a bullet might. The hot guns had to be cooled regularly. Many men might have been overcome by the heat if I hadn't taken pitchers of water to them. I made many trips from the spring where I filled the pitcher to the thirsty troops.

Molly Pitcher No. 2: The Battle of Monmouth in June 1778 was the worst. The heat was terrible, and besides bringing water I helped drag a

From *Whose Tale Is True?: Readers Theatre to Introduce and Research 49 Amazing American Women* by Nancy Polette. Westport, CT: Teacher Ideas Press. Copyright © 2008.

wounded man to safety. Then, to my horror, I saw William fall.

Molly Pitcher No. 3: I ran to my husband and saw that he had been overcome by the heat. There was no one else around. The British were upon us. I picked up the rammer, shoved it into the cannon, and fired. I fired again and again, and the British were driven off.

Host: Weren't you afraid of being caught in the middle of the battle?

Molly Pitcher No. 1: There was no time to be afraid. I knew the enemy had to be defeated. There was no one else to fire the cannon.

Molly Pitcher No. 2: The enemy fire was so heavy on that October day that I knew I had a job to do. I just kept firing. There was no time to be afraid.

Molly Pitcher No. 3: General Washington credited me with winning the battle. He made me a noncommissioned officer, and the men called me "Sergeant Molly." It was the proudest moment of my life.

Host: Now it is time to decide whose tale is true. We will vote by a show of hands. Is it No. 1? Is it No. 2? Is it No. 3? Now for the moment you have all been waiting for:

Will the real Molly Pitcher step forward?

Answer: No. 3

No. 1 mentioned a six shooter, which had not yet been invented.

No. 2 first said the Battle of Monmouth took place in June. Later she said it took place in October.

FURTHER READING

Bertanzetti, Eileen. *Molly Pitcher, Heroine.* Chelsea House, 2002.

Stevenson, Augusta. *Molly Pitcher, Young Patriot.* Macmillan, 1960.

From *Whose Tale Is True?: Readers Theatre to Introduce and Research 49 Amazing American Women* by Nancy Polette. Westport, CT: Teacher Ideas Press. Copyright © 2008.

REPORTING ON MOLLY PITCHER

Suppose you were present at the Battle of Monmouth with Molly Pitcher. Fill in the boxes to tell what you would experience. Use the information in the five senses poem in the second half of the form.

Colors	Sounds	Sights
_____	_____	_____
_____	_____	_____
_____	_____	_____

Smells	Tastes	Feelings
_____	_____	_____
_____	_____	_____
_____	_____	_____
_____	_____	_____

Five Senses Poem

Line

1-Color   The Monmouth Battlefield was painted _____

2-Sound   It sounded like _____

3-Taste   It tasted like _____

4-Smell   It smelled like _____

5-Sight   It looked like _____

6-Feeling   It made Molly Pitcher feel like _____

Martha Washington (1731–1802)

The First "First Lady"

Reading Parts: Host, Martha Washington No. 1, Martha Washington No. 2, Martha Washington No. 3

Host: [facing audience] Welcome to "Whose Tale Is True?" Each of our three guests claims to be Martha Washington, wife of George Washington. Only one, however, is telling the complete truth. It is up to you to decide which one is the real Martha Washington. Now let's meet our guests. [facing readers] Welcome. Can you tell us something about yourselves?

Martha Washington No. 1: I was born in 1731 on a plantation owned by my father. He believed strongly in education for girls, and I learned reading and writing as well as Greek and Latin.

Martha Washington No. 2: Growing up on a plantation was sometimes work and sometimes fun. I learned to cook and sew and run a household. I became quite a good horsewoman. Once I rode my horse up the stairs in my uncle's home.

Martha Washington No. 3: I was the oldest daughter of my parents and always very small for my age. I never grew taller than five feet. I learned at an early age how to run a large household.

Host: I understand that you were quite young when you married.

Martha Washington No. 1: I was the oldest daughter of my parents, and like other girls of my time had almost no schooling other than in domestic and social skills. I married at age 18. My first husband was quite wealthy, but I had been taught how to manage our many servants.

Martha Washington No. 2: I did marry at age 18, but became a widow at age 26. My husband, Daniel Park Custis, passed away in 1757.

Martha Washington No. 3: Eighteen was not a young age for marriage at the time I lived. My husband was well-to-do, so I had more free time than many wives. Because I never learned to read, I enjoyed listening to the radio.

From *Whose Tale Is True?: Readers Theatre to Introduce and Research 49 Amazing American Women* by Nancy Polette. Westport, CT: Teacher Ideas Press. Copyright © 2008.

Host: How did you feel about being the First Lady of the Land?

Martha Washington No. 1: I married George Washington two years after my first husband's death. My greatest concern was his comfort and happiness. I went with him to many battlegrounds to look after him properly. I never dreamed of becoming the first lady.

Martha Washington No. 2: I was with George at Valley Forge. When there was a spare moment, George and I would take winter rides together. It was rough living, but not nearly as stressful as life as the president's wife. Sometimes I felt like a state prisoner. Fancy teas and dressing up were not for me.

Martha Washington No. 3: I became the first lady when George was elected president in 1789. I never enjoyed all the parties and ceremonies that went with the job. I was most happy in 1797 when George and I left public life to return to Mount Vernon.

Host: Now it is time to decide whose tale is true. We will vote by a show of hands. Is it No. 1? Is it No. 2? Is it No. 3? Now for the moment you have all been waiting for:

Will the real Martha Washington step forward?

Answer: No. 2.

No. 1 contradicted herself about her schooling.

No. 3 mentioned radios, which did not exist in the 1700s.

FURTHER READING

Anderson, LaVere. *Martha Washington: First Lady of the Land.* Gerrard, 1973.

Wagoner, Jean. *Martha Washington: America's First Lady.* Macmillan, 1992.

REPORTING ON MARTHA WASHINGTON

Fill in the missing words and sing the Martha Washington song to the tune of "My Bonnie Lies Over the Ocean."

There once was a young girl named (1) M_____

Most people said she was quite (2) s_____

She once rode a horse up a (3) s_____

Though she was a mere five feet tall

Chorus

(4)M _____ (5)M _____

She learned how to spin and to cook and sew

(6)M _____ (7)M _____

She wondered where her life would go.

At 25 she was a (8) w_____

With two (9) c_____ and an estate

George Washington asked her to marry

She said yes and they set a date.

Repeat Chorus

Then George led the people to freedom

They chose him to be (10) p_____

And Martha became the (11) f_____ l_____

She followed wherever he went.

Now Martha did not like her new role

It was quite a change in her (12) l_____

She wanted to go to (13) M_____ V_____

And just be a simple housewife.

Answer Key: 1-Martha; 2-small; 3-staircase; 4, 5, 6, 7-Martha; 8-widow; 9-children; 10-president; 11-first lady; 12-life; 13-Mount Vernon

From *Whose Tale Is True?: Readers Theatre to Introduce and Research 49 Amazing American Women* by Nancy Polette. Westport, CT: Teacher Ideas Press. Copyright © 2008.

Dolley Payne Todd Madison (1768–1849)

Saving the White House Treasures

Reading Parts: Host, Dolley Madison No. 1, Dolley Madison No. 2, Dolley Madison No. 3

Host: [facing audience] Welcome to "Whose Tale Is True?" Each of our three guests claims to be Dolley Madison, wife of President James Madison. Only one, however, is telling the complete truth. It is up to you to decide which one is the real Dolley Madison. Now let's meet our guests. [facing readers] Welcome. I understand that you were raised in a family with strong religious values.

Dolley Madison No. 1: My family was of the Quaker faith and closely followed the dictates of the faith. Our clothing was very dark and sober, and my parents often frowned at me when I laughed more than I should.

Dolley Madison No. 2: People always said I had a happy personality and a warm heart. I had many suitors, but chose John Todd as my husband when I was 22. He was a doctor who was much in demand by his patients.

Dolley Madison No. 3: My family was strict but loving. I was well prepared to be a wife an mother. I married John Todd in 1790 and we had one son. John died three years later in a yellow fever epidemic.

Host: How did you come to meet and marry James Madison?

Dolley Madison No. 1: James was a representative from Virginia when we met. It was love at first sight even though he was much older than I. Ours was a happy marriage both during and after our time in the White House. People asked how I could marry such a sober man who never smiled. I told them our hearts understood each other.

Dolley Madison No. 2: After John Todd, my lawyer husband, died I discarded the somber clothing I had worn for so long. The new me caught the attention of James Madison, and we were married in 1794.

Dolley Madison No. 3: My first marriage was short but happy. When my first husband died, I knew it was up to me to raise our sons and I did the best I could. I felt that James Madison would be a good father to the boys, and that was one reason I married him even though he was 17 years older than I.

Host: We understand that you once saved the White House treasures. Can you tell us about that?

Dolley Madison No. 1: It was during the War of 1812. James had left the White House to confer with his officers. Word had come that the British were marching on Washington.

Dolley Madison No. 2: I was just sitting down to my supper when a young man came with a note from my husband. The note said that I must leave the White House at once. The British were near. Everyone else was gone. I had only old John, our faithful servant, and the young messenger to help gather important papers and valuable pieces of art.

Dolley Madison No. 3: I knew that many White House treasures could be saved if we acted quickly. I directed Old John and the messenger to load the wagons with those things I chose, including the portrait of George Washington. We barely escaped when the British entered the White House and burned it to the ground.

Host: Now it is time to decide whose tale is true. We will vote by a show of hands. Is it No. 1? Is it No. 2? Is it No. 3? Now for the moment you have all been waiting for:

Will the real Dolley Madison step forward?

Answer: No. I

No. 2 contradicted herself, saying first her husband was a doctor and then saying he was a lawyer.

No. 3 contradicted herself. First she said she had one son, then that she had several sons.

FURTHER READING

Anthony, Katherine. *Dolley Madison: Her Life and Times.* Doubleday, 1949.

Barzman, Sol. *The First Ladies.* Cowles, 1970.

REPORTING ON FIRST LADIES

Use this pattern to compare Dolley Madison and Martha Washington.

If I were Dolley Madison

As a child I _____

As a young woman I _____

I married _____

As first lady I spent much of my time _____

_____

I was admired for _____

And was happy when _____

But I didn't _____

Because Martha Washington did that.

If I were Martha Washington

As a child I _____

As a young woman I _____

I married _____

As first lady I spent much of my time _____

_____

I was admired for _____

And was happy when _____

But I didn't _____

Because Dolley Madison did that.

From *Whose Tale Is True?: Readers Theatre to Introduce and Research 49 Amazing American Women* by Nancy Polette. Westport, CT: Teacher Ideas Press. Copyright © 2008.

Part Two

Nineteenth Century

Sacagawea (1790–1884?)

Trailblazer

Reading Parts: Host, Sacagawea No. 1, Sacagawea No. 2, Sacagawea No. 3

Host: [facing audience] Welcome to "Whose Tale Is True?" Each of our three guests claims to be Sacagawea, who traveled with Lewis and Clark on their journey to the Pacific. Only one, however, is telling the complete truth. It is up to you to decide which one is the real Sacagawea. Now let's meet our guests. [facing readers] Welcome. I understand that your life has not been an easy one. Is that true?

Sacagawea No. 1: That is true. I did have a happy childhood in my Indian village, but that changed when I was kidnapped by Hidasta warriors.

Sacagawea No. 2: I thought the warriors might keep me as a servant in their village, but instead they sold me to a fur trapper named Charbonneau.

Sacagawea No. 3: Charbonneau paid 50 French pesos for me. I became his wife and bore him a son. He treated me well. It was a much better life than being a servant in a Hidasta village.

Host: How did you come to travel with Lewis and Clark?

Sacagawea No. 1: Lewis and Clark paid Charbonneau to be their guide. They wanted me and our son along in case we met any Indians along the way. Clark thought the Indians might be friendly if they saw me and the child.

Sacagawea No. 2: Since I could speak English, I often served as a translator. On the trip we met a band of Shoshone. The leader was my brother. I was happy to see him once again.

Sacagawea No. 3: I was a valuable member of the expedition. In addition to acting as a translator, I found food for the party, cooked, and mended clothes.

Host: How were you treated by the other members of the expedition?

From *Whose Tale Is True?: Readers Theatre to Introduce and Research 49 Amazing American Women* by Nancy Polette. Westport, CT: Teacher Ideas Press. Copyright © 2008.

Sacagawea No. 1: I was treated well. I believe they appreciated my skills. I was given a vote along with the men when anything important had to be decided.

Sacagawea No. 2: The expedition soon realized what a valuable member I was. As a translator I did not speak English but would speak my native language to Charbonneau. He would translate it into French for another member of the party, who would give the message in English to Lewis and Clark.

Sacagawea No. 3: The expedition made it all the way to the Pacific Ocean. On the return journey my husband and I left the expedition when we reached the Missouri River. I lived out the rest of my life on a Shoshone Reservation.

Host: Now it is time to decide whose tale is true. We will vote by a show of hands. Is it No. 1? Is it No. 2? Is it No. 3? Now for the moment you have all been waiting for:

Will the real Sacagawea step forward?

Answer: No. 3

No. 1 said she was paid for in French pesos. The peso is a Spanish currency, not a French one.

No. 2 first said she spoke English and later said she did not speak English.

FURTHER READING

Polette, Nancy. *Sacajawea.* Children's Press, 2003.

Sandford, William. *Sacagawea.* Enslow, 1997.

Seymour, Flora. *Sacagawea: American Pathfinder.* Macmillan, 1991.

From *Whose Tale Is True?: Readers Theatre to Introduce and Research 49 Amazing American Women* by Nancy Polette. Westport, CT: Teacher Ideas Press. Copyright © 2008.

REPORTING ON SACAGAWEA

Pretend you are traveling with Sacagawea on the Lewis and Clark expedition. Complete the pattern that follows, detailing the sights you see on the journey.

ON THE TRAIL, COME WITH ME

WONDROUS SIGHTS YOU WILL SEE

(List sights you would see if you were Sacagawea)

_____

_____

_____

_____

_____

SIGHTS GALORE, HERE ARE MORE

(List four or five more sights)

_____

_____

_____

_____

_____

WHERE AM I?

WITH THE LEWIS AND CLARK EXPEDITION, OF COURSE

From *Whose Tale Is True?: Readers Theatre to Introduce and Research 49 Amazing American Women* by Nancy Polette. Westport, CT: Teacher Ideas Press. Copyright © 2008.

Harriet Tubman (1820–1913)

Black Moses

Reading Parts: Host, Harriet Tubman No. 1, Harriet Tubman No. 2, Harriet Tubman No. 3

Host: [facing audience] Welcome to "Whose Tale Is True?" Each of our three guests claims to be Harriet Tubman, conductor on the Underground Railroad. Only one, however, is telling the complete truth. It is up to you to decide which one is the real Harriet Tubman. Now let's meet our guests. [facing readers] Welcome. What can you tell us about your early life?

Harriet Tubman No. 1: I was born a slave on a plantation in Maryland. I had 10 brothers and sisters, and we all were expected to do the master's bidding or feel the lash. Even though life was hard, when we heard we were to be sent to the deep South we knew life would be even harder there.

Harriet Tubman No. 2: When a slave tried to escape from the plantation, he was tied up like an animal and beaten. When I was 12 my face showed how angry I was to see a tied up slave, and the overseer hit me on the head with a shovel. I felt the effects of that blow the rest of my life.

Harriet Tubman No. 3: When my brothers and I heard that the master's slaves were to be sent South, we knew we had to escape. Not far into the woods my brothers turned back for fear they would be caught. I kept on walking to freedom.

Host: Why didn't you turn back with your brothers? Weren't you afraid of getting caught?

Harriet Tubman No. 1: As an only child my mother tried to hide me from the cruelty of the master, but that didn't keep me from getting my head hit with a shovel. My choice was escaping to freedom or remaining a slave. I chose freedom.

Harriet Tubman No. 2: I was 25 years old in 1849 when I escaped from the plantation. President Abraham Lincoln hadn't yet signed the Fugitive Slave Act. It seemed as good a time as any to escape.

Harriet Tubman No. 3: A neighbor gave me names and directions to a safe house. I was passed along from house to house on the Underground Railroad until I reached freedom in Philadelphia. Then and there I vowed to use the Underground Railroad to free my parents.

Host: Tell us about your work on the Underground Railroad.

Harriet Tubman No. 1: I used the Railroad to return to the plantation twice, first to free three of my brothers and sisters and then to free my parents.

Harriet Tubman No. 2: Altogether I made 19 trips to help other slaves find the road to freedom. Along the Railroad friends provided safe hiding places, food, and clothing for the runaway slaves.

Harriet Tubman No. 3: I led more than 300 slaves to freedom and never lost a "passenger." Once a slave agreed to make the journey there was no turning back. A live runaway could do great harm by going back.

Host: Host: Now it is time to decide whose tale is true. We will vote by a show of hands. Is it No. 1? Is it No. 2? Is it No. 3? Now for the moment you have all been waiting for:

Will the real Harriet Tubman step forward?

Answer: No. 3

No. 1 first said she was one of 11 children, then said she was an only child.

No. 2 was wrong: Lincoln was not president in 1849 and did not sign the Fugitive Slave Act of 1850.

FURTHER READING

Adler, David. *A Picture Book of Harriet Tubman*. Holiday House, 1992.

Ferris, Jeri. *Go Free or Die: A Story of Harriet Tubman*. Carolrhoda, 1988.

Schraff, Anne. *Harriet Tubman: Moses of the Underground Railroad*. Enslow, 2001.

From *Whose Tale Is True?: Readers Theatre to Introduce and Research 49 Amazing American Women* by Nancy Polette. Westport, CT: Teacher Ideas Press. Copyright © 2008.

I WISH I WERE

Find information about a famous African American. You might choose George Washington Carver, Sojourner Truth, Ida Wells, Martin Luther King Jr., or any other. Follow the pattern below to report the information you find.

Pattern

Line one: I wish I were:

Line two: State who you want to be

Line three: Tell one major accomplishment

Line four: Tell how the accomplishment was achieved

Line five: Provide additional information.

Example

I wish I were:

Harriet Tubman,

Leading 300 slaves to safety on the Underground Railroad,

Accepting shelter, food, and clothing from friends and supporters,

And never losing a single "passenger."

Your Turn

I wish I were:

_____

_____

_____

_____

From *Whose Tale Is True?: Readers Theatre to Introduce and Research 49 Amazing American Women* by Nancy Polette. Westport, CT: Teacher Ideas Press. Copyright © 2008.

Clara Barton (1821–1912)

Founder of the American Red Cross

Reading Parts: Host, Clara Barton No. 1, Clara Baron No. 2, Clara Barton No. 3

Host: [facing audience] Welcome to "Whose Tale Is True?" Each of our three guests claims to be Clara Barton, the battlefield nurse who founded the American Red Cross. Only one, however, is telling the complete truth. It is up to you to decide which one is the real Clara Barton. Now let's meet our guests. [facing readers] Welcome. You must be a real go-getter to have accomplished as much as you have.

Clara Barton No. 1: My parents would laugh to hear you say that. I have always been painfully shy. When I was born in 1821 I was the youngest of five children. My mother used to worry because I was such a shrinking violet. As a young woman I had no formal training as a nurse, but I nursed my ill brother for two years.

Clara Barton No. 2: I did not attend school but was educated at home. When I was 15 years old I took a teaching job in New Jersey. I commuted by bus from my home to the school. I saw many children whose parents could not afford to send them to a private school, so I started a free public school

Clara Barton No. 3: By the time I was 40 years old I had a job in the Patent Office in Washington, D.C. This was a terrible time for the nation, when the North and South went to war. While working in the nation's capital I became aware of the desperate need for medical supplies for our troops.

Host: Is that how you became known as a battlefield nurse?

Clara Barton No. 1: Because I was trained as a nurse, I saw my job as getting the medical supplies to where they were needed. When I arrived at the battlefields with wagons of supplies I saw the terrible shortage of medical people. I did what I could to help.

From *Whose Tale Is True?: Readers Theatre to Introduce and Research 49 Amazing American Women* by Nancy Polette. Westport, CT: Teacher Ideas Press. Copyright © 2008.

Clara Barton No. 2: I was so successful in getting supplies where they were needed that I was granted a pass to travel with the ambulances. Sometimes I had to bully men along the way to get help to the battlefields.

Clara Barton No. 3: I tended the wounded at Antietam, Manassas, and Fredricksburg. After the war I headed a bureau to search for missing men. We were able to identify 12,000 men who died at Andersonville.

Host: How did the American Red Cross come about?

Clara Barton No. 1: In 1869 I went to Switzerland to serve as a nurse during the Franco–Prussian War. I saw the fine work that was being done there by the International Red Cross of Europe.

Clara Barton No. 2: I was determined that the United States should take part in the Red Cross work. The government refused to listen to my pleas until the Geneva Treaty was signed in 1882.

Clara Barton No. 3: The American Red Cross was established, and I became its first president. It was my idea to extend Red Cross services to any group of people who face calamity. One of our first civilian efforts was helping those caught in the Jamestown flood in 1889.

Host: Now it is time to decide whose tale is true. We will vote by a show of hands. Is it No. 1? Is it No. 2? Is it No. 3? Now for the moment you have all been waiting for:

Will the real Clara Barton step forward?

Answer: No. 3

No. 1 contradicted herself, stating first that she had no formal nursing training, then that she was a trained nurse.

No. 2 could not have ridden on a bus. There were no busses in the 1800s.

FURTHER READING

Quackenbush, Robert. *Clara Barton & Her Victory Over Fear.* Simon & Schuster, 1995.

Stevenson, Augusta. *Clara Barton: Founder of the American Red Cross.* Macmillan, 1962.

REPORTING ON CLARA BARTON

Find evidence in the script to support the following statements:

Clara Barton was shy.

_____

_____

Clara Barton was a responsible person.

_____

_____

Clara Barton was stubborn.

_____

_____

Clara Barton cared about others.

_____

_____

Clara Barton was a woman of courage.

_____

_____

Clara Barton was determined.

_____

_____

From *Whose Tale Is True?: Readers Theatre to Introduce and Research 49 Amazing American Women* by Nancy Polette. Westport, CT: Teacher Ideas Press. Copyright © 2008.

Louisa May Alcott (1832–1888)

Author

Reading Parts: Host, Louisa May Alcott No. 1, Louisa May Alcott No. 2, Louisa May Alcott No. 3

Host: [facing audience] Welcome to "Whose Tale Is True?" Each of our three guests claims to be the well-known writer, Louisa May Alcott. Only one, however, is telling the complete truth. It is up to you to decide which one is the real Louisa May Alcott. Now let's meet our guests. [facing readers] Welcome. Tell us what led you to become a writer.

Louisa May Alcott No. 1: I was born in 1832 and grew up in Concord, Massachusetts. My father was a teacher and instilled in me and my sisters a love of literature. I began keeping a journal and writing about my daily activities at an early age.

Louisa May Alcott No. 2: It is true that father was a teacher, but he was also a dreamer, and his get-rich schemes kept us as poor as church mice. As soon as I was old enough I got a job as the weather girl at the local television station. Sometimes I got to write the news stories, and this led to my interest in writing.

Louisa May Alcott No. 3: One of father's schemes was a communal farm, and he had me and my sisters hoeing and planting and running the tractor 10 to 12 hours a day. There was no time for writing. I didn't begin writing seriously until the farm failed and we moved back to town.

Host: I understand you were in your early thirties when the Civil War began. Did you play any role in the war?

Louisa May Alcott No. 1: Yes. During the Civil War I served as an army nurse, and this resulted in my first published work. I wrote about my experiences in *Hospital Sketches.*

Louisa May Alcott No. 2: During the war women were not allowed to serve in any capacity. I just stayed home and prayed for all of the soldiers that we knew.

Louisa May Alcott No. 3: I interviewed many of the soldiers from the North when they returned from battle. This resulted in my popular novel, *Little Men*.

Host: Is *Little Women* based on your life and that of your family?

Louisa May Alcott No. 1: The novel is partly based on my life, but many of the incidents are fictional. I learned from authors who were frequent visitors to our home how to write an exciting story. These visitors were Ralph Waldo Emerson, Henry David Thoreau, and Nathaniel Hawthorne, all friends of my father.

Louisa May Alcott No. 2: Yes, every word is true. Everything in the book happened to me or my family.

Louisa May Alcott No. 3: Not one word is true. The whole novel came from my imagination.

Host: Now it is time to decide whose tale is true. We will vote by a show of hands. Is it No. 1? Is it No. 2? Is it No. 3? Now for the moment you have all been waiting for:

Will the real Louisa May Alcott step forward?

Answer: No. 1

No. 2 mentioned television, which did not exist in the 1800s.

No. 3 mentioned tractors, which did not exist in the 1800s.

FURTHER READING

Aller, Susan. *Beyond Little Women: The Story of Louisa May Alcott.* Carolrhoda, 2004.

FAMOUS WRITERS

Louisa May Alcott met several very famous writers who visited her home when she was growing up in Concord, Massachusetts. Place the initials of each writer before his works.

Ralph Waldo Emerson   RWE
Nathaniel Hawthorne   NH
Henry David Thoreau   HDT

1. _____ *Civil Disobedience*

2. _____ *Nature*

3. _____ *The Scarlet Letter*

4. _____ *Walden, or Life in the Woods*

5. _____ *Self-Reliance*

6. _____ *The House of the Seven Gables*

7. _____ *Twice-Told Tales*

Which writer do you think must influenced Louisa May Alcott's writing?

_____

Why? _____

_____

_____

_____

_____

_____

Answer Key: Emerson-2, 5; Hawthorne-3, 6, 7; Thoreau-1, 4

Charlotte Forten Grimke (1837–1914)

One of the First to Teach Former Slaves

Reading Parts: Host, Charlotte Forten No. 1, Charlotte Forten No. 2, Charlotte Forten No. 3

Host: [facing audience] Welcome to "Whose Tale Is True?" Each of our three guests claims to be Charlotte Forten, abolitionist and one of the first to teach former slaves. Only one, however, is telling the complete truth. It is up to you to decide which one is the real Charlotte Forten. Now let's meet our guests. [facing readers] Welcome. How did you get such a fine education that it enabled you to teach others, when no blacks were allowed in Philadelphia schools?

Charlotte Forten No. 1: I came from a wealthy family and had every advantage as a child. Because the Philadelphia schools would not admit Negroes, I was taught at home by private tutors. I never attended a regular school.

Charlotte Forten No. 2: My grandfather had amassed a fortune of more than $100,000, so I was taught by private tutors at home until I was 16. Then I was the first black person to be admitted to an integrated school in Salem, Massachusetts.

Charlotte Forten No. 3: My family had no money, so I taught myself to read by finding books that had been thrown away. I especially liked fantasies such as *The Hobbit* and *The Lion, the Witch and the Wardrobe*.

Host: How did you become a teacher of former slaves on the Sea Island off the Carolina coast?

Charlotte Forten No. 1: After I graduated with honors from the Salem Normal School I was told that the government was looking for teachers for slaves who had fled to the safety of the Sea Islands. I volunteered.

Charlotte Forten No. 2: Life was not easy on the Sea Islands when I answered the government's call to teach there. Housing was poor, and there were dirt and fleas. I carried a pistol because of the hatred of the few Southerners who remained on the island. We

From *Whose Tale Is True?: Readers Theatre to Introduce and Research 49 Amazing American Women* by Nancy Polette. Westport, CT: Teacher Ideas Press. Copyright © 2008.

had to depend on gifts of teaching materials for our 140 pupils. The government supplied nothing.

Charlotte Forten No. 3: The oppressive heat of the Sea Islands was almost too much to bear. Yet the work that I and another teacher did was so important that we could not leave. We were proud of our students when they sang "My Country 't'is of Thee" when the Emancipation Proclamation was read to them.

Host: What do you believe is the greatest gift you gave your students?

Charlotte Forten No. 1: The gift of believing in themselves. Southerners who say the race is inferior should see the readiness with which these children learn and understand.

Charlotte Forten No. 2: The greatest gift anyone can receive is a love of reading. In one year I read more than 100 books, from the classics to poetry, and these I shared with my students.

Charlotte Forten No. 3: As the first Salem School graduate to volunteer, I encouraged many others to follow in my footsteps so that the children would always have teachers. This turned out well and the children, who were so eager to learn, were never without instruction.

Host: Now it is time to decide whose tale is true. We will vote by a show of hands. Is it No. 1? Is it No. 2? Is it No. 3? Now for the moment you have all been waiting for:

Will the real Charlotte Forten Grimke step forward?

Answer: No. 2

No. 1 contradicted herself by saying she had never attended a regular school, yet she graduated from one.

No. 3 was an avid reader but could not have read *The Lion, The Witch and the Wardrobe* because it was not published until after her lifetime.

FURTHER READING

Burchard, Peter. *Charlotte Forten: A Black Teacher in the Civil War.* Crown, 1995.

Douty, Esther Morris. *Charlotte Forten, Free Black Teacher.* Garrard Publishing, 1971.

Longsworth, Polly. *I, Charlotte Forten, Black and Free.* Thomas Y. Crowell, 1970.

From *Whose Tale Is True?: Readers Theatre to Introduce and Research 49 Amazing American Women* by Nancy Polette. Westport, CT: Teacher Ideas Press. Copyright © 2008.

FIND SOMEONE WHO . . .

During Charlotte Forten's time on the Sea Islands she lived in fear that Confederate soldiers might attack. Find out what members of your class know about the Civil War. Put a classmate's name after any item for which he or she can give the correct answer. You can only use a name one time. The student who first finds a different name with a correct answer for each line is the winner.

FIND SOMEONE WHO KNOWS:

1. The year the Civil War began _____

Name _____

2. The year the Civil War ended _____

Name _____

3. The number of states that formed the Confederacy _____

Name _____

4. The chief crop of the South in 1860 _____

Name _____

5. The year John Brown raided Harper's Ferry _____

Name _____

6. The president of the Confederacy _____

Name _____

7. The year Lincoln became president of the United States _____

Name _____

☞ **Answer Key:** 1-1861; 2-1865; 3-11; 4-cotton; 5-1859; 6-Jefferson Davis; 7-1861

Elizabeth Blackwell (1821–1910)

The First Woman Physician

Reading Parts: Host, Elizabeth Blackwell No. 1, Elizabeth Blackwell No. 2, Elizabeth Blackwell No. 3

Host: [facing audience] Welcome to "Whose Tale Is True?" Each of our three guests claims to be Elizabeth Blackwell, the first woman doctor in the United States Only one, however, is telling the complete truth. It is up to you to decide which one is the real Elizabeth Blackwell. Now let's meet our guests. [facing readers] Welcome. How did you go from running a boarding school to becoming the first woman physician?

Elizabeth Blackwell No. 1: From childhood I had dreamed of becoming a doctor, but in the time I lived a woman was not expected to have a career. A woman's job was to look after her husband and children. I never had a husband or children, and I was determined to make my dream come true.

Elizabeth Blackwell No. 2: My father died when I was a teenager. I had eight brothers and sisters, and to support the family my sisters and I ran a boarding school. That didn't stop me from studying medicine with the local doctor. I learned all about proven remedies, MRIs, and surgery.

Elizabeth Blackwell No. 3: While running the boarding school, every minute I could spare was spent studying medicine with a local doctor. I learned a great deal but knew I had to go to medical school to become a real doctor. I wanted especially to meet the needs of women's health problems.

Host: What happened when you applied to the medical colleges?

Elizabeth Blackwell No. 1: I was rejected by every school to which I applied. I was determined to be accepted for a full course of study but was turned down by every one.

Elizabeth Blackwell No. 2: I was getting pretty discouraged, then I got an acceptance from the Geneva Medical College in New York. I found out

From *Whose Tale Is True?: Readers Theatre to Introduce and Research 49 Amazing American Women* by Nancy Polette. Westport, CT: Teacher Ideas Press. Copyright © 2008.

later that the administration asked the students to vote on my admittance as a joke. The joke was on the administration. The students voted yes!

Elizabeth Blackwell No. 3: I entered the medical college but was treated as an outcast. I was not allowed to watch surgery or dissections simply because I was a woman. After a time a few of the students did accept me. I graduated first in the class in January 1849.

Host: Did the public accept you as a doctor of medicine?

Elizabeth Blackwell No. 1: Before going into private practice I wanted to learn more. I went to Paris for further study and while there contracted an infection, which left me blind in one eye. I gave up my goal of being a surgeon and returned to New York.

Elizabeth Blackwell No. 2: I had a hard time setting up my practice. Landlords did not want to rent office space to me, so I had to buy a house and see patients there. I also set up a dispensary in the New York City slums to treat people who had no doctor.

Elizabeth Blackwell No. 3: My work in the slums was greatly appreciated. My practice was confined to treating children, which had always been my goal. I never married, but in 1854 I adopted a child. I also went on a lecture tour of Great Britain, and my adopted daughter went with me. In 1859 I was the first woman to have my name on the British Medical Register.

Host: Now it is time to decide whose tale is true. We will vote by a show of hands. Is it No. 1? Is it No. 2? Is it No. 3? Now for the moment you have all been waiting for:

Will the real Elizabeth Blackwell step forward?

Answer: No. 1

No. 2 mentioned MRIs, which did not exist in the 1800s

No. 3 contradicted herself, first saying she wanted to treat women, then that her goal was to treat children.

FURTHER READING

Greene, Carol. *Elizabeth Blackwell.* Children's Press, 1994.

Henry, Joanne. *Elizabeth Blackwell: Girl Doctor.* Simon & Schuster, 1996.

From *Whose Tale Is True?: Readers Theatre to Introduce and Research 49 Amazing American Women* by Nancy Polette. Westport, CT: Teacher Ideas Press. Copyright © 2008.

REPORTING ON ELIZABETH BLACKWELL

Circle the letter under T of the statement is true.

Circle the letter under F if the statement is false.

Place the circled letters on the lines at the bottom of the page.

The word they spell tells something about Elizabeth Blackwell.

	T	F
1. Elizabeth Blackwell came from a wealthy family.	K	S
2. She studied medicine while teaching school.	T	L
3. She was accepted to several medical schools.	M	U
4. Geneva College students thought her acceptance was a joke.	B	C
5. She was allowed to watch operations.	N	B
6. She graduated last in her class.	B	O
7. Landlords did not want to rent space to her.	R	P
8. She was married twice.	S	N

_____ _____ _____ _____ _____ _____ _____ _____

From *Whose Tale Is True?: Readers Theatre to Introduce and Research 49 Amazing American Women* by Nancy Polette. Westport, CT: Teacher Ideas Press. Copyright © 2008.

Annie Oakley (Phoebe Anne Oakley Moses) (1860–1926)

Extraordinary Sharpshooter

Reading Parts: Host, Annie Oakley No. 1, Annie Oakley No. 2, Annie Oakley No. 3

Host: [facing audience] Welcome to "Whose Tale Is True?" Each of our three guests claims to be Annie Oakley, world famous sharpshooter. Only one, however, is telling the complete truth. It is up to you to decide which one is the real Annie Oakley. Now let's meet our guests. [facing readers] Welcome. I understand that you learned to handle a gun at a very early age.

Annie Oakley No. 1: That is true. I was born in a log cabin in the Ohio wilderness. We were very poor. My father died when I was five years old. I had eight brothers and sisters to be fed, so I took my father's gun and headed for the woods.

Annie Oakley No. 2: I got to be a pretty good shot. There would not have been much to eat otherwise. My family was very poor. What little money we had I got by selling extra meat to the store.

Annie Oakley No. 3: When I was 15 I entered my first shooting contest. I competed against Frank Butler, a champion shooter, and won by one shot. Frank didn't mind. In fact, a few years later we got married.

Host: Did you give up shooting contests after you were married?

Annie Oakley No. 1: Oh, no. Frank and I entered many contests together. I continued to send my prize money home to help my mother feed my six brothers and sisters. Frank and I gave lots of shooting demonstrations. Crowds really went wild when I shot a cigarette out of Frank's mouth.

From *Whose Tale Is True?: Readers Theatre to Introduce and Research 49 Amazing American Women* by Nancy Polette. Westport, CT: Teacher Ideas Press. Copyright © 2008.

Annie Oakley No. 2: Buffalo Bill offered me a part in his show. He thought I needed a catchy name. Because my family were Quakers and I liked Quaker Oats for breakfast, I named myself Annie Oakley.

Annie Oakley No. 3: I traveled with Buffalo Bill's Wild West Show for 17 years. I could shoot a dime tossed in the air. I could hit the thin edge of a playing card standing 90 feet away. I was always tiny, five feet tall. Folks wondered how I could enter the arena waving that heavy rifle in the air.

Host: Was it true that a train wreck cut your career short?

Annie Oakley No. 1: Yes. I was badly injured in a train wreck in 1901 when I was 41 years old. For a time I was partly paralyzed and thought I would never perform again.

Annie Oakley No. 2: I was badly injured, but I couldn't let the folks in Oakley, Ohio, down. After all, I took my stage name from that town. I worked hard to recover, and my shooting was as good as ever.

Annie Oakley No. 3: After the accident I didn't tour as much, but I continued to enter shooting contests. I also trained soldiers to shoot during World War I. At age 62 I shot 100 clay pigeons without missing.

Host: Now it is time to decide whose tale is true. We will vote by a show of hands. Is it No. 1? Is it No. 2? Is it No. 3? Now for the moment you have all been waiting for:

Will the real Annie Oakley step forward?

Answer: No. 3

No. 2 contradicted herself about the number of her brothers and sisters.

No. 3 contradicted herself about how she chose her stage name.

FURTHER READING

Krensky, Stephen. *Shooting for the Moon: The Amazing Life and Times of Annie Oakley.* Melanie Kroupa Books, 2001.

Ruffin, Frances. *Annie Oakley.* Powerkids Press, 2002.

REPORTING ON ANNIE OAKLEY

Fill in the blanks, one letter per blank.

1. Annie's real last name was _____ _____ S_____ _____ .

2. Her father died when she was _____ I _____ _____ years old.

3. At age eight she shot game and sold it to the local _____ _____ _____ R _____ .

4. She entered her first shooting contest at age ____ _____ _____ ____ E ____ _____ .

5. She married _____ _____ A _____ _____ Butler.

6. She appeared in Buffalo Bill's _____ _____ L _____ W _____ _____ _____ _____ H _____ ____ .

7. In 1901 she was badly hurt in a ____ _____ _____ I _____ wreck.

8. She trained _____ _____ _____ _____ _____ E _____ _____ to shoot.

9. She was only _____ _____ _____ E feet tall.

Write one sentence telling what you remember most about Annie Oakley.

_____

_____

_____

_____

Answer Key: 1-Moses; 2-five; 3-store; 4-fifteen; 5-Frank; 6-Wild West Show; 7-train; 8-soldiers; 9-five

Calamity Jane (Martha Jane Canary) (1852–1903)

She-Devil of the Yellowstone

Reading Parts: Host, Calamity Jane No. 1, Calamity Jane No. 2, Calamity Jane No. 3

Host: [facing audience] Welcome to "Whose Tale Is True?" Each of our three guests claims to be Calamity Jane, the "She-Devil of the Yellowstone." ' Only one, however, is telling the complete truth. It is up to you to decide which one is the real Calamity Jane. Now let's meet our guests. [facing readers] Welcome. I read that you were born in Missouri. How did you end up in the Wild West?

Calamity Jane No. 1: Yes, I was born in Princeton, Missouri, in 1852. When my mother died, my Pa and brothers decided to try to strike it rich in the silver mines near Virginia City. That was when the first calamity happened.

Calamity Jane No. 2: The Indians didn't like the settlers moving onto their land, and I was separated from my father and brothers in an Indian uprising. I was 10 years old, and there was nobody to phone back East to come and get me, so I was on my own.

Calamity Jane No. 3: For the next 10 years I got by as best I could. Having no mother to guide me, I wore men's clothing, chewed tobacco, and learned to be a pretty good shot. I could never stay in one place very long. For 40 years I traveled all over the West, from Arizona through the Dakota Territories.

Host: Is it true that you were a scout for the U.S. Army?

Calamity Jane No. 1: It sure is. When I was near 20 years old General Cook appointed me a scout. I was willing to go places others were afraid to go. Wild Bill Hickok was my boss. He knew I was up to any challenge. I think it's kind of nice that our final resting places are near each other in Deadwood, South Dakota.

Calamity Jane No. 2: It was while I was an army scout that I got my nickname. I was scouting in South Dakota when my captain was surrounded by Indians. Captain Egan was wounded and had fallen off his horse. I rode in, picked him up, and got out of there. He's the one named me Calamity Jane.

Calamity Jane No. 3: I really didn't think the name, Calamity, fit. I not only saved Captain Egan, but I saved six passengers in a runaway stage coach traveling from Deadwood to Wild Birch. The driver was wounded and the coach was out of control. I jumped from my horse to the driver's seat and got things under control.

Host: I think the folks in Deadwood, South Dakota, would not call you Calamity, would they?

Calamity Jane No. 1: Probably not. You see, when I arrived there they were in the middle of a smallpox epidemic. I did what I could to help. The folks were so grateful that a few years later they wanted to have a big party to honor me, but by that time I was at my final resting place in Arizona.

Calamity Jane No. 2: I was a Pony Express rider for a time, and my route ran 50 miles, from Deadwood to Custer. The Deadwood folks knew their mail would get through because robbers along the trail knew I was a crack shot. There were no calamities when I carried the mail.

Calamity Jane No. 3: When Wild Bill Hickok wrote about me, he said I was remembered as a "saint" by the folks in Deadwood because of my help during the smallpox epidemic. Most folks would laugh at that idea. I was a rough riding, rough talking woman, and as good a shot as any man. I went where I pleased and did what I pleased, and maybe along the line I did help a few folks out.

Host: Now it is time to decide whose tale is true. We will vote by a show of hands. Is it No. 1? Is it No. 2? Is it No. 3? Now for the moment you have all been waiting for:

Will the real Calamity Jane step forward?

Answer: No. 3

No. 1 first said she was buried in Deadwood, South Dakota, and then said she was buried in Arizona.

No. 2 mentioned telephones, which had not yet been invented.

FURTHER READING

Faber, Doris. *Calamity Jane, Her Life and Legend.* Houghton Mifflin, 1992.

Sanford, William. *Calamity Jane: Frontier Original.* Enslow, 1996.

From *Whose Tale Is True?: Readers Theatre to Introduce and Research 49 Amazing American Women* by Nancy Polette. Westport, CT: Teacher Ideas Press. Copyright © 2008.

PREPARE A NEWSPAPER CLIPPING REPORT

Find pictures, articles, or ads in the newspaper that are related to the life of Calamity Jane in some way. Look carefully at the paper for several days.

Find and clip the items listed below. As you find other items, list them on lines 9 through 15. Share your clipping report with the class.

1. A picture of a new town

2. A headline that deals with a possible epidemic

3. An article about a pioneer in any field

4. An event that could take place only in a free society

5. The price of an ounce of gold

6. An article about mail delivery or the post office

7. A picture of someone who looks like he/she might belong in the Wild West

8. An advertisement for something Calamity Jane would like to have

9. _____

10. _____

11. _____

12. _____

13. _____

14. _____

15. _____

From *Whose Tale Is True?: Readers Theatre to Introduce and Research 49 Amazing American Women* by Nancy Polette. Westport, CT: Teacher Ideas Press. Copyright © 2008.

Madame C. J. Walker (1867–1919)

Inventor/Businesswoman

Reading Parts: Host, Madame C. J. Walker No. 1, Madame C. J. Walker No. 2, Madame C. J. Walker No. 3

Host: [facing audience] Welcome to "Whose Tale Is True?" Each of our three guests claims to be Madame C. J. Walker, inventor and business woman. Only one, however, is telling the complete truth. It is up to you to decide which one is the real Madame Walker. Now let's meet our guests. [facing readers] Welcome. Tell us about your early life. We understand that your family was not wealthy.

Madame C. J. Walker No. 1: My parents were former slaves. As a young woman I picked cotton and worked as a laundress and cook to make ends meet. I was married at 14, widowed at 20, and had a child to support.

Madame C. J. Walker No. 2: I was married in 1881 at age 14. At age 20 I became a widow. I had to work hard to earn money to buy my parents' freedom from slavery. I worked as a field hand, cook, and laundress.

Madame C. J. Walker No. 3: When my husband died in 1887 I moved to St. Louis, working as a laundress and going to school at night. While in St. Louis I heard a radio show about a bald woman and got an idea to start a business selling hair products.

Host: What kind of hair products did you sell?

Madame C. J. Walker No. 1: About the time we moved to St. Louis my hair started falling out. I had a dream that told me what ingredients to mix. I mixed those ingredients, and the mixture stopped my hair loss.

Madame C. J. Walker No. 2: My hair loss formula was such a success that I began selling it door to door. Some women asked if I had any-

Madame C. J. Walker No. 3: thing that would straighten hair. I used my kitchen as a laboratory and developed a successful method for straightening hair. My products spread by word of mouth.

Madame C. J. Walker No. 3: I invented the formula to stop hair loss in my kitchen, and it was so successful that I moved to Denver, Colorado, in 1905 and opened my first factory there. I employed dozens of salespeople to take the products on the road.

Host: I have read that your Indianapolis factory employed 5,000 Negro women.

Madame C. J. Walker No. 1: That is correct. I also believed in giving back to the community. I gave thousands of dollars to the Tuskegee Institute, the NAACP, and other black charities.

Madame C. J. Walker No. 2: My daughter helped to run some of the factories, leaving me time to develop new products and supervise sales. My hard work paid off, and I became a millionaire.

Madame C. J. Walker No. 3: I moved to New York City in 1916 but continued to oversee the business and run the New York office. My sales agents were successful because I organized them into clubs, with prizes for those with the greatest sales.

Host: Now it is time to decide whose tale is true. We will vote by a show of hands. Is it No. 1? Is it No. 2? Is it No. 3? Now for the moment you have all been waiting for:

Will the real Madame C. J. Walker step forward?

Answer: No. 1

No. 2 mentioned buying her parents' freedom. They were already free in 1881.

No. 3 mentioned the radio, which did not exist in 1887.

FURTHER READING

Lasky, Katherine. *Vision of Beauty*. Candlewick Press, 2000.

McKissack, Patricia. *Madame C. J. Walker: Self-Made Millionaire*. Enslow, 2001.

From *Whose Tale Is True?: Readers Theatre to Introduce and Research 49 Amazing American Women* by Nancy Polette. Westport, CT: Teacher Ideas Press. Copyright © 2008.

HOMONYMS!

Write four sentences about Madame C. J. Walker using a pair of the homonyms listed below in each sentence. Check meanings in the dictionary.

weak	wade	waive	ware
week	weighed	wave	where
we'll	wail	wear	weather
wheel	whale	where	whether
wood	waist	wait	wet
would	waste	weight	whet

Example: In one **week** she stirred up several **weak** batches of hair growth formula.

1. _____

_____

_____

2. _____

_____

_____

3. _____

_____

_____

4. _____

_____

_____

From *Whose Tale Is True?: Readers Theatre to Introduce and Research 49 Amazing American Women* by Nancy Polette. Westport, CT: Teacher Ideas Press. Copyright © 2008.

Jane Addams (1860–1935)

Guardian of the Poor

Reading Parts: Host, Jane Addams No. 1, Jane Addams No. 2, Jane Addams No. 3

Host: [facing audience] Welcome to "Whose Tale Is True?" Each of our three guests claims to be Jane Addams, founder of the first settlement house for the poor. Only one, however, is telling the complete truth. It is up to you to decide which one is the real Jane Addams. Now let's meet our guests. [facing readers] Welcome. We know you are from a wealthy family. What caused you to have such an interest in the poor?

Jane Addams No. 1: In the 1880s more and more immigrants were pouring into Chicago. Most had a hard time getting jobs because few spoke English. I thought I might use some of my family's money to set up a laboratory where immigrants could be taught computer skills. That way they would have a chance at a job.

Jane Addams No. 2: In the mid- to late 1800s wealthy families sent their sons and daughters abroad to travel Europe for a year. While I was in London I visited a settlement house that provided services for the poor. It gave me the idea to start a similar settlement house in Chicago.

Jane Addams No. 3: I thought about the plight of the poor for many years. Finally in 1889, when I was 50 years old, I decided to help poor immigrants learn English by opening Hull House, a place where they could come for help.

Host: How successful was Hull House?

Jane Addams No. 1: Immigrants were reluctant to come to Hull House that first year. We never had more than one or two a day.

Jane Addams No. 2: Hull House was an immediate success. The first year 5,000 of Chicago's poor came through our doors. Immigrants were eager to learn English, and we had volunteers to teach them.

Jane Addams No. 3: We also had a nursery school, housing for working girls, a community kitchen, and vocational training.

Host: Hull House sounds like a very ambitious project. It doesn't sound like you had time to support any other causes.

Jane Addams No. 1: Oh, but I did! My friend Ellen Starr helped me start Hull House and took over the day-to-day chores of running it. That left me free to fight for women's right to drive an automobile. In my day only men were allowed to drive.

Jane Addams No. 2: I supported many worthy causes, including world peace, factory inspections, an eight-hour working day for women, and voting rights for women. For my support of these and other causes, and especially for the founding of Hull House, I was awarded the Nobel Peace Prize in 1931.

Jane Addams No. 3: In the time that I lived, women were not allowed to vote, and I worked for many years to get the vote for women. I made banners, gave speeches, wrote newspaper articles, and sponsored a nationwide bus tour to take the women's right to vote to the people.

Host: Now it is time to decide whose tale is true. We will vote by a show of hands. Is it No. 1? Is it No. 2? Is it No. 3? Now for the moment you have all been waiting for:

Will the real Jane Addams step forward?

Answer: No. 2

No. 1 mentioned computers, which did not exist in the 1800s.

No. 3 said she started Hull House in 1889 at the age of 50. In 1889 she would have been 29 years old.

FURTHER READING

Fradin, Judith. *Jane Addams, Champion of Democracy*. Clarion, 2006.

Kishel, Ann Marie. *Jane Addams: A Life of Cooperation*. Lerner, 2006.

Raatma, Lucia. *Jane Addams*. Compass Point Books, 2006.

WORKER MATCH

To keep Hull House running smoothly, Jane Addams needed the services of many different workers.

Match the worker she might have called for help with the job that he did.

1. _____ cooper   A. made spoons and other tableware

2. _____ cutler   B. made clothing and hats

3. _____ farrier   C. made planks for flooring

4. _____ founder   D. made barrels out of wood

5. _____ miller   E. made wagons and carriages

6. _____ milliner   F. sharpened knives

7. _____ sawyer   G. ground wheat for bread

8. _____ silversmith   H. made brass candlesticks

9. _____ wainright   I. made things out of tin

10. _____ whitesmith   J. made horseshoes

Answer Key: 1-D; 2-F; 3-J; 4-H; 5-G; 6-B; 7-C; 8-A; 9-E; 10-I

Mary Eliza Mahoney (1845–1926)

The First African American Registered Nurse

Reading Parts: Host, Mary Mahoney No. 1, Mary Mahoney No. 2, Mary Mahoney No. 3

Host: [facing audience] Welcome to "Whose Tale Is True?" Each of our three guests claims to be Mary Maloney, the first black graduate nurse. Only one, however, is telling the complete truth. It is up to you to decide which one is the real Mary Maloney. Now let's meet our guests. [facing readers] Welcome. I am sure that becoming the first African American registered nurse in this country was not an easy task. When did you decide to take on the challenge?

Mary Mahoney No. 1: I was born in 1845, the oldest child in a family of 25. In a family that large I had plenty of practice fixing cuts, scrapes, and broken bones as well as taking care of my brothers and sisters when they became ill. Nursing just seemed to be a natural career for me to pursue.

Mary Mahoney No. 2: In addition to nursing my brothers and sisters, I took a job as a cook at the New England Hospital for Women and Children. I watched a lot of nurses go about their duties and knew that was what I wanted to do.

Mary Mahoney No. 3: At the New England Hospital where I worked for 15 years I was not only a nurse but a maid and weatherwoman as well. There was a lady doctor at the hospital who started a program to train nurses. Fortunately for me she believed in equal rights for women and blacks, and I was accepted into the program.

Host: Tell us about the nurses' training program.

Mary Mahoney No. 1: We were expected to work 16 hours a day, 7 days a week. The work was hard. We scrubbed floors, changed beds, washed dishes, ironed, transported patients for CAT scans, went to classes, and studied in between.

From *Whose Tale Is True?: Readers Theatre to Introduce and Research 49 Amazing American Women* by Nancy Polette. Westport, CT: Teacher Ideas Press. Copyright © 2008.

Mary Mahoney No. 2: Dr. Marie Zakrzewska was head of the school, and her standards for graduating were high. When the 16 months were up only 3 out of the 40 original applicants graduated. I am happy to say that I was one of the three.

Mary Mahoney No. 3: One reason that I stuck with the rigorous program was my age. I was 33 when I was accepted into nursing school and knew if I did not make it through there would never be another chance. I would be cooking and scrubbing the rest of my life.

Host: After graduation, did you work in a hospital?

Mary Mahoney No. 1: Part of our training took us into homes as a private duty nurse. I decided that this was what I wanted to do. I worked for 40 years as a private duty nurse. As a professional nurse I impressed upon my patients that my duty was to care for them and that I was not employed to do household tasks.

Mary Mahoney No. 2: As a professional nurse I was a co-founder of the National Association of Colored Graduate Nurses. Later on the association created an award in my honor, and I was eventually inducted into the Nursing Hall of Fame.

Mary Mahoney No. 3: My graduation from the nursing program of the New York Hospital for Women and Children was the highlight of my life. My diploma was worth every floor I scrubbed and every bed I made. I then began my professional nursing career as a private duty nurse.

Host: Now it is time to decide whose tale is true. We will vote by a show of hands. Is it No. 1? Is it No. 2? Is it No. 3? Now for the moment you have all been waiting for:

Will the real Mary Eliza Mahoney step forward?

Answer: No. 2

No. 1 mentioned CAT scans, which had not yet been invented.

No. 3 was confused about which hospital sponsored her nurse's training.

FURTHER READING

Miller, Helen S. *Mary Eliza Mahoney: America's First Black Professional Nurse.* Wright Group, 1986.

REPORTING ON MARY ELIZA MAHONEY

Cut the story strips apart. Have eight players each draw a slip, line up in the order in which the events took place, and tell Mary's story.

1. She worked 16 hours a day, 7 days a week.

2. Mary Mahoney was born in 1845.

3. She co-founded the National Association of Colored Graduate Nurses.

4. She worked as a hospital maid and cook for 15 years.

5. She worked as a private duty nurse.

6. Mary took care of her 24 brothers and sisters.

7. Mary was one of three nurses to graduate.

8. Mary entered the nursing program.

✂ **Answer Key:** 2, 6, 4, 1, 8, 7, 5, 3

From *Whose Tale Is True?: Readers Theatre to Introduce and Research 49 Amazing American Women* by Nancy Polette. Westport, CT: Teacher Ideas Press. Copyright © 2008.

Susan B. Anthony (1820–1906)

Fighter for Women's Rights

Reading Parts: Host, Susan B. Anthony No. 1, Susan B. Anthony No. 2, Susan B. Anthony No. 3

Host: [facing audience] Welcome to "Whose Tale Is True?" Each of our three guests claims to be Susan B. Anthony, defender of women's rights. Only one, however, is telling the complete truth. It is up to you to decide which one is the real Susan B. Anthony. Now let's meet our guests. [facing readers] Welcome. Did your family have anything to do with your desire for justice for all?

Susan B. Anthony No. 1: When I was born in 1820, my parents were Quakers who believed in leading simple lives. We always dressed plainly in dark colors, and joking and laughter were frowned upon. Justice was an important idea in our home.

Susan B. Anthony No. 2: My Quaker parents taught us the meaning of justice in our early years. Many of the Quakers provided shelter for slaves traveling on the Underground Railroad. They considered owning another person to be a terrible injustice.

Susan B. Anthony No. 3: In 1820, when I was born, there were many injustices. Slavery was legal. A woman's earnings belonged to her husband. Women were not allowed to vote. Perhaps that is why I became a rabble-rouser.

Host: Tell us about your life as a rabble-rouser.

Susan B. Anthony No. 1: One of the first causes I fought for was passing laws to make drinking alcohol illegal. I organized the Women's State Temperance Society of New York. At a time when women were not encouraged to speak in public, I gave a lot of speeches.

Susan B. Anthony No. 2: My Methodist upbringing taught me at a young age that slavery was wrong. I thought Abraham Lincoln was a fine president and hoped that many of the groups I spoke to had an effect on his issuing of the Emancipation Proclamation.

Susan B. Anthony No. 3: Once the slavery issue was decided, I took up the cause of women's right to vote. I even tried to vote before any laws were passed allowing women to do so. I was arrested and spent a short time in jail.

Host: It sounds like leading the fight for women's rights was not an easy task.

Susan B. Anthony No. 1: It disturbed me that women were not allowed to attend universities. I wore myself out flying from one city to another to face angry crows. I knew that until women received more education, they would never receive other rights that they should have.

Susan B. Anthony No. 2: I talked the University of Rochester into admitting women if I could raise $50,000. I had no problem raising the money. The university officials were surprised, but they had to admit women.

Susan B. Anthony No. 3: I did not live long enough to see women get the vote, but I believe my efforts helped to bring this about. I know that my magazine, *Revolution*, was read all over the country and made people think about the many injustices done to women.

Host: Now it is time to decide whose tale is true. We will vote by a show of hands. Is it No. 1? Is it No. 2? Is it No. 3? Now for the moment you have all been waiting for:

Will the real Susan B. Anthony step forward?

Answer: No. 3

No. 1 mentioned flying. The airplane had not yet been invented.

No. 2 stated that she was raised as a Quaker, then later stated that her childhood religion was Methodist.

FURTHER READING

Dumbeck, Kristina. *Leaders of Women's Suffrage.* Lucent Books, 2001.

Klingel, Cynthia Fitterer. *Susan B. Anthony: Reformer.* Child's World, 2003.

REPORTING ON SUSAN B. ANTHONY

Use the information about Susan B. Anthony to match the items below.

1. _____ Her birthdate A. rabble-rouser

2. _____ Her religion jail

3. _____ What her parents taught vote

4. _____ What she called herself Quaker

5. _____ Took slaves to freedom angry crowds

6. _____ President she admired University of Rochester

7. _____ Where she spent a short time Lincoln

8. _____ First to admit women justice

9. _____ What she faced 1820

10. _____ What she wanted for women Underground Railroad

Answer Key: 1-I; 2-D; 3-H; 4-A; 5-J; 6-G; 7-B; 8-F; 9-E; 10-C

From *Whose Tale Is True?: Readers Theatre to Introduce and Research 49 Amazing American Women* by Nancy Polette. Westport, CT: Teacher Ideas Press. Copyright © 2008.

Mary Harris Jones (1830–1930)

The Miner's Angel

Reading Parts: Host, Mary Harris Jones No. 1, Mary Harris Jones No. 2, Mary Harris Jones No. 3

Host: [facing audience] Welcome to "Whose Tale Is True?" Each of our three guests claims to be Mary Harris Jones, who devoted her life to getting better working conditions for miners and children. Only one, however, is telling the complete truth. It is up to you to decide which one is the real Mary Harris Jones. Now let's meet our guests. [facing readers] Welcome. Do you think you really deserve the title "The most hated woman in America?"

Mary Harris Jones No. 1: Only the mine owners called me that. The miners themselves called me Mother Jones. In getting better wages for the hard-working miners I did ruffle a few feathers. The mine owners were not too fond of me.

Mary Harris Jones No. 2: I was proud of that title because it meant that my plea for better wages for the miners was being heard. Another crusade I led was to get little children out of factories. The factory owners weren't too happy with me about that.

Mary Harris Jones No. 3: Can you imagine a little child being forced to work at a machine for 12 hours a day? If the child got hurt, as many of them did, there was no help or compensation. I thought this was wicked and did what I could to all attention to these abuses.

Host: What got you interested in the labor movement?

Mary Harris Jones No. 1: After I lost my husband and children in the epidemic of 1872, I went to Chicago and opened a dressmaking shop. I often went to rich folks' houses to sew, and while I sat in the fancy houses working I could see hungry children out on the street. I knew it was either the street or the factory for them, and that they needed help. I went on television to plead for help for the children.

From *Whose Tale Is True?: Readers Theatre to Introduce and Research 49 Amazing American Women* by Nancy Polette. Westport, CT: Teacher Ideas Press. Copyright © 2008.

Mary Harris Jones No. 2: When my dressmaking shop burned, I stayed with friends who belonged to the Knights of Labor. Their talk about the plight of the coal miners led me to want to do something about it.

Mary Harris Jones No. 3: Thanks to Mrs. O'Leary's cow, my dressmaking shop burned down. I stayed with friends who belonged to the Knights of Labor. It bothered me that all they did was talk about the problems of the working man. I was determined to do more than talk.

Host: What specifically did you do?

Mary Harris Jones No. 1: Wherever there was a strike, I was there helping the workers. I organized and ran educational meetings. In 1890 I became an organizer for the United Mine Workers.

Mary Harris Jones No. 2: In 1912 I organized the miners' wives to keep their husbands from returning to work until a decent wage was set. I led a march of crippled children to the president's Long Island home so he could see what happens to little children forced to work in factories.

Mary Harris Jones No. 3: In 1913 there was violence during one strike in Virginia, and I was arrested and sentenced to 20 years in jail. I was 83 years old, and President Clinton put pressure on Governor Hatfield to set me free. It has been a hard life, but I believe my efforts have bettered workers' lives everywhere.

Host: Now it is time to decide whose tale is true. We will vote by a show of hands. Is it No. 1? Is it No. 2? Is it No. 3? Now for the moment you have all been waiting for:

Will the real Mary Harris Jones step forward?

Answer: No. 2

No. 1 mentioned being on television, which did not exist until the late 1940s.

No. 3 mentioned President Clinton, who was not president until long after her death.

FURTHER READING

Kraft, Betsy. *Mary Harris Jones: One Woman's Fight for Labor.* Clarion, 1995.

Rappaport, Doreen. *Trouble at the Mines.* Thomas Y. Crowell, 1987.

REPORTING ON MARY HARRIS JONES

Complete the report card for Mary Harris Jones. Give her a grade in each area. In the section for notes, tell why you believe the grade is fair.

GRADED IN	GRADE	NOTES
RESPONSIBILITY		
COMPASSION		
WORKS WELL WITH OTHERS		
FOLLOWS THROUGH ON ASSIGNMENTS		
CREATIVITY		

From *Whose Tale Is True?: Readers Theatre to Introduce and Research 49 Amazing American Women* by Nancy Polette. Westport, CT: Teacher Ideas Press. Copyright © 2008.

Emily Dickinson (1830–1886)

American Lyrical Poet

Reading Parts: Host, Emily Dickinson No. 1, Emily Dickinson No. 2, Emily Dickinson No. 3

Host: [facing audience] Welcome to "Whose Tale Is True?" Each of our three guests claims to be Emily Dickinson, one of America's most famous poets. Only one, however, is telling the complete truth. It is up to you to decide which one is the real Emily Dickinson. Now let's meet our guests. [facing readers] Welcome. Many biographers have called you a sad lady. Were you always an unhappy person?

Emily Dickinson No. 1: Not at all. As a young girl I grew up in a family that believed in education for women. My father was a lawyer and also treasurer of Amherst College. He saw to it that I was well educated. I enjoyed my school years and had many friends.

Emily Dickinson No. 2: As a young girl I attended Amherst Academy. In 1847 I was also a student at the Mount Holyoke Seminary. I especially enjoyed the literature courses, in which we read the poetry of Robert Browning, John Keats, and Shel Silverstein.

Emily Dickinson No. 3: Even though I enjoyed my courses of study, I left Mount Holyoke after one year. I missed home too much. Most people would say I was homesick.

Host: What caused you to withdraw from the world?

Emily Dickinson No. 1: There has been a lot of speculation about my becoming a recluse. Some writers have said I fell in love with the Reverend Charles Wadsworth and was heartsick when he left for the West Coast. Others have said that I greatly admired another gentleman, Samuel Bowles. I have never divulged the reason I did not marry and will not do so now.

Emily Dickinson No. 2: I lived for many years with my sister, Lavinia, and saw little need for contact with the outside world. Even though I was not well educated, I enjoyed writing poetry. My greatest companion was my notebook. I never actually counted, but I think I wrote more than 1,800 poems.

Emily Dickinson No. 3: I never revealed to the world the reason I became a recluse. I simply stopped leaving the house and saw few visitors. My life was in my poetry. I loved children and would send treats down to them in a basket from my window. I never spoke to them, but I wrote about their joyful play in my poems.

Host: Did you ever believe that you would become one of the world's most famous poets?

Emily Dickinson No. 1: Of course not. I wrote poems simply to express my thoughts. I never intended for them to be read by others.

Emily Dickinson No. 2: I never wanted to share my poems with others. I made my sister, Lavinia, promise to burn all of the poems after my death. She kept her promise by making copies and burning all of the originals. Then she had all 500 of my poems published.

Emily Dickinson No. 3: I had no idea that others would find pleasure in my poetry. I am glad I was not around when the first book of my poetry was published. I am sure that my lifetime output of 500 poems would make it a very large book.

Host: Now it is time to decide whose tale is true. We will vote by a show of hands. Is it No. 1? Is it No. 2? Is it No. 3? Now for the moment you have all been waiting for:

Will the real Emily Dickinson step forward?

Answer: No. 2

No. 1 mentioned Shel Silverstein, who had not yet been born in the 1800s.

No. 3 first said she had written more than 1,800 poems and later said she wrote 500.

FURTHER READING

Herstek, Amy. *Emily Dickinson: Solitary and Celebrated Poet.* Enslow, 2003.

Winter, Jeanette. *Emily Dickinson's Letters to the World.* Frances Foster Books, 2002.

From *Whose Tale Is True?: Readers Theatre to Introduce and Research 49 Amazing American Women* by Nancy Polette. Westport, CT: Teacher Ideas Press. Copyright © 2008.

REPORTING ON EMILY DICKINSON

Emily Dickinson was a world famous poet. Describe her using the bio-poem model that follows.

Line 1. Name   _____

Line 2. Like what flower?   _____

Line 3. Like what song?   _____

Line 4. Who cares deeply about   _____

Line 5. Who avoids   _____

Line 6. Who needs   _____

Line 7. Who gives   _____

Line 8. Who fears   _____

Line 9. Who would like to see   _____

Line 10. Resident of   _____

From *Whose Tale Is True?: Readers Theatre to Introduce and Research 49 Amazing American Women* by Nancy Polette. Westport, CT: Teacher Ideas Press. Copyright © 2008.

Nellie Bly (1867–1922)

Investigative Reporter

Reading Parts: Host, Nellie Bly No. 1, Nellie Bly No. 2, Nellie Bly No. 3

Host: [facing audience] Welcome to "Whose Tale Is True?" Each of our three guests claims to be Nellie Bly, a daring woman reporter whose greatest hoax was to get herself committed to an insane asylum. Only one, however, is telling the complete truth. It is up to you to decide which one is the real Nellie Bly. Now let's meet our guests. [facing readers] Welcome. What can you tell us about your childhood?

Nellie Bly No. 1: My real name is Elizabeth Cochrane. I was born in 1867. My father died when I was six years old, leaving my mother and 14 brothers and sisters to get by as best we could.

Nellie Bly No. 2: After my father died there were many days we did not know where the next meal was coming from. I did go to school, but I never made the honor roll. The only thing that interested me was writing.

Nellie Bly No. 3: When I was growing up there was an airport near our house. I used to watch the planes take off and wish that I was making the trip. When I was 16 I did leave home, to seek work in Philadelphia. I found that only low-paying jobs were available to women.

Host: How was it then that you got a job as a reporter on a major newspaper?

Nellie Bly No. 1: I read an article in the *Pittsburgh Dispatch* that said women were only good for housework and raising children. It made me mad!

Nellie Bly No. 2: I was so mad that I wrote a letter to the editor of the paper. The editor wrote back asking me what I would write if I were a journalist. I told him, and he hired me to write about women's lives. I knew I could do a good job. After all, I was an A student all through school.

Nellie Bly No. 3: The editor thought I needed a pen name, and he named me Nellie Bly. I didn't mind. It sounded sort of catchy. I was determined to write real news stories, so I became an undercover reporter.

Host: What were some of your most famous stories?

Nellie Bly No. 1: By 1887 I was writing for the *New York World*. I wrote about the terrible housing conditions in New York City. I also wrote about poverty and harmful labor practices.

Nellie Bly No. 2: I heard rumors about the awful treatment of mental patients on Blackwell Island, so I pretended to be a mental patient and got firsthand information about the terrible conditions there. Conditions improved considerably after my news story was published.

Nellie Bly No. 3: Perhaps my most famous stories were those I sent back from all over the world when I went around the world in 72 days, 6 hours, 11 minutes, and 14 seconds. I was met by a huge crowd on my return to New York.

Host: Now it is time to decide whose tale is true. We will vote by a show of hands. Is it No. 1? Is it No. 2? Is it No. 3? Now for the moment you have all been waiting for:

Will the real Nellie Bly step forward?

Answer: No. 1

No. 2 said she was not a good student but then said she made all As.

No. 3 mentioned airplanes, which had not yet been invented.

FURTHER READING

Christensen, Bonnie. *The Daring Nellie Bly*. Knopf, 2003.

Krensky, Stephen. *Nellie Bly: A Name to Be Reckoned With*. Aladdin Books 2003.

A NELLIE BLY CHANT

Find 13 short facts about Nellie Bly. Write them on the lines below. Each fact should have no more than three syllables. The first two lines are done for you. When all lines are complete, read the Nellie Bly chant.

Facts About Nellie Bly
Nellie Bly
Brave woman

_____

_____

_____

_____

These are just a few

_____

_____

_____

_____

_____

_____, too.

From near and far
Here they are
Facts about Nellie Bly!

Ida B. Wells (Barnett) (1862–1931)

Crusader with a Pen

Reading Parts: Host, Ida B. Wells No. 1, Ida B. Wells No. 2, Ida B. Wells No. 3

Host: [facing audience] Welcome to "Whose Tale Is True?" Each of our three guests claims to be Ida B. Wells, crusader with a pen. Only one, however, is telling the complete truth. It is up to you to decide which one is the real Ida B. Wells. Now let's meet our guests. [facing readers] Welcome. You were known in your time as a crusading editor. Why was that?

Ida B. Wells No. 1: In 1875 Congress passed a law that said all people, regardless of race, could ride any public transportation. I refused to give up my seat on the train and bit a conductor who tried to force me to do so. I was dragged off the train by two baggage handlers. I sued the railroad and won. That was the beginning of my being a crusader.

Ida B. Wells No. 2: I had always been disturbed at the unjust punishments given African Americans and decided to do something about it. I became a partner in the newspaper *Free Speech*. In articles I wrote in the paper I said that if the city could not protect the Negro from lynchings, then the Negroes should leave town. A lot did.

Ida B. Wells No. 3: After reading my articles, many Negro refused to patronize white-owned businesses. This made the business owners mad.

Host: Did you continue to write about the many injustices you saw?

Ida B. Wells No. 1: Three of my friends were lynched for no reason. My earlier lawsuit against the railroad was thrown out of court. I could not stop writing. My articles made folks so mad that they destroyed our newspaper office. My life was in danger.

Ida B. Wells No. 2: I had to leave Memphis and move to Chicago. There I continued my attacks on the unjust treatment of Negroes in the South. I went on television several times to let the people of Chicago know what was going on.

Ida B. Wells No. 3: In Chicago I continued my antilynching campaign. I also worked hard for women to get the vote and took part in the 1913 march in Washington, D.C., as well as fighting against segregated schools.

Host: Is it correct that you retired in 1895?

Ida B. Wells No. 1: Yes and no. In 1895 I married Attorney F. L. Barnett. Married women were not expected to work in those days, and I planned to retire from journalism and care for my new husband and home.

Ida B. Wells No. 2: I found I could not give up the fight for justice. In 1909 I was one of the founding members of the National Association for the Advancement of Colored People. Even within the organization they called me a "radical" when I could not agree with many of the ideas of the leaders.

Ida B. Wells No. 3: In 1930 I ran for a seat in the Illinois State Legislature. I was one of the first black women ever to do so. I did not win, but I put up a good fight and a lot of my views were heard.

Host: Now it is time to decide whose tale is true. We will vote by a show of hands. Is it No. 1? Is it No. 2? Is it No. 3? Now for the moment you have all been waiting for:

Will the real Ida B. Wells step forward?

Answer: No. 3

No. 1 said at first she won a lawsuit against the railroad and then said she did not win.

No. 2 mentioned television, which had not yet been invented.

FURTHER READING

Moore, Heidi. *Ida B. Wells Barnett*. Heinemann, 2004.

Welch, Catherine. *Ida B. Wells Barnett: Powerhouse with a Pen*. Carolrhoda Books, 2000.

FACTS ABOUT IDA B. WELLS

Ida B. Wells risked her life to write about the injustices toward African American. Write a news story about the day that her newspaper office was destroyed.

Most Important News

What happened _____

_____

When did it happen? _____

What was involved? _____

_____

_____

Important Details

_____

_____

_____

_____

Less Important Details

_____

_____

_____

_____

_____

From *Whose Tale Is True?: Readers Theatre to Introduce and Research 49 Amazing American Women* by Nancy Polette. Westport, CT: Teacher Ideas Press. Copyright © 2008.

Ida Tarbell (1857–1944)

She Fought an Oil Giant

Reading Parts: Host, Ida Tarbell No. 1, Ida Tarbell No. 2, Ida Tarbell No. 3

Host: [facing audience] Welcome to "Whose Tale Is True?" Each of our three guests claims to be Ida Tarbell, investigative reporter. Only one, however, is telling the complete truth. It is up to you to decide which one is the real Ida Tarbell. Now let's meet our guests. [facing readers] Welcome. Tell us how a little girl who grew up on the western Pennsylvania oil frontier became one of the nation's best-known reporters.

Ida Tarbell No. 1: The oil frontier was rough, but my mother was every inch a lady. She made sure that I had a good education. I never intended to be a journalist. I wanted to be a biologist, but there were no jobs for women in that field, so I became a teacher.

Ida Tarbell No. 2: I had a childhood filled with adventure growing up near the Pennsylvania oil fields. My mother hated those years. She said the town of Rouseville was too rough. She was delighted when we moved to Titusville, which she said was a more civilized town.

Ida Tarbell No. 3: My mother insisted that I attend Allegheny College. I graduated and taught school for two years, until I decided that teaching wasn't for me. I was able to go to France for graduate work and to support myself I wrote articles for newspapers and magazines and eventually became a full-time writer for *McClure Magazine*.

Host: What got you interested in the Rockefeller oil empire?

Ida Tarbell No. 1: Growing up as an orphan around the Pennsylvania oil fields, I often heard hard luck tales from those who had lost their land and oil wells to the strong-arm tactics of the Rockefeller empire. I decided to research the Standard Oil Company to see if any of the tales were true.

Ida Tarbell No. 2: My father, who manufactured wooden oil tanks, lost his business when his prices were undercut by the Rockefellers. This meant lean times for our family

From *Whose Tale Is True?: Readers Theatre to Introduce and Research 49 Amazing American Women* by Nancy Polette. Westport, CT: Teacher Ideas Press. Copyright © 2008.

Ida Tarbell No. 3: I was always interested in the way big businesses operated. After doing painstaking research into the oil industry and the unethical tactics of the Rockefellers, I wrote a series of articles that exposed the ruthless practices of the Standard Oil Trust, which controlled 95 percent of all the oil produced in the United States. My series led Congress to investigate and was partly responsible for the passage of the Sherman Anti-Trust Act.

Host: The *New York Times* called you one of the " Twelve Greatest American Women." How did you feel about that?

Ida Tarbell No. 1: Because journalism was a man's profession and there were so few women reporters, it wasn't difficult to stand out. I paid little attention to labels.

Ida Tarbell No. 2: I did not concern myself with what others said. I started the *American Magazine*, where I was free to interview anyone and to write on the issues of the day without a boss looking over my shoulder. I think my frank approach to issues helped other reporters to take on more difficult assignments.

Ida Tarbell No. 3: I was too busy bringing important issues to the public's attention to worry about being a famous woman. In 1918 I wrote a number of articles about the plight of working women. In 1922 I wrote about the bad influence of rock music on our youth. My job as I saw it was to awaken the public conscience.

Host: Now it is time to decide whose tale is true. We will vote by a show of hands. Is it No. 1? Is it No. 2? Is it No. 3? Now for the moment you have all been waiting for:

Will the real Ida Tarbell step forward?

Answer: No. 2

No. 1 first said her mother influenced her education, then said she was an orphan.

No. 3 mentioned rock music, which did not exist at that time.

FURTHER READING

Conn, Frances. *Ida Tarbell, Muckraker*. Thomas Nelson, 1872.

Paradis, Adrian. *Ida Tarbell, Pioneer Woman Journalist and Biographer*. Children's Press, 1985.

REPORTING ON IDA TARBELL

When a small person takes on a giant, it is quite a sight to see. Ida Tarbell took on the wealthy Rockefellers and the giant oil industry.

Complete the poem that follows with facts about Ida Tarbell.

I am Ida Tarbell

Come to my home in _____

See my _____

Hear my _____

Read my _____

I am Ida Tarbell

Watch others _____ toward me

Watch while I _____

I am Ida Tarbell. Visit me, hear me, see me, but watch out,

I may be watching you

Challenge

How many similarities can you find between the story of Ida Tarbell and the story of David and Goliath?

From *Whose Tale Is True?: Readers Theatre to Introduce and Research 49 Amazing American Women* by Nancy Polette. Westport, CT: Teacher Ideas Press. Copyright © 2008.

Part Three

Twentieth Century

Margaret Tobin (Maggie or "Molly") Brown (1867–1932)

She Was Unsinkable

Reading Parts: Host, Molly Brown No. 1, Molly Brown No. 2, Molly Brown No. 3

Host: [facing audience] Welcome to "Whose Tale Is True?" Each of our three guests claims to be Molly Brown, survivor of the *Titanic*. Only one, however, is telling the complete truth. It is up to you to decide which one is the real Molly Brown. Now let's meet our guests. [facing readers] Welcome. We have heard that yours is a "rags to riches" story. Is this true?

Molly Brown No. 1: You bet! I was born in Hannibal, Missouri, in 1867. My father's small salary at the gas works never stretched far enough to take care of our family of eight. I went to work in the local tobacco factory at age 13 to help out.

Molly Brown No. 2: Our house only had one bedroom, and there was me, my Ma and Pa, and five brothers and sisters. We had no fancy clothes for school, so my aunt taught us reading and math. I loved reading.

Molly Brown No. 3: We were so poor that I worked as a waitress and in a tobacco factory to help out. When I was still in my teens, my brother and I heard tales about striking it rich out West. We took off together for Leadville, Colorado.

Host: Did you strike it rich?

Molly Brown No. 1: Not the way you think. I didn't find a gold mine, but I did snag a husband. For a time we lived in a two-room cabin. Then James was able to solve some problems at the Little Johnny Mine, and he made a lot of money. We moved to Denver and built a mansion.

Molly Brown No. 2: Life in Denver was a lot different from Leadville. We had a big house, gave lots of parties, and gave money to lots of charities. We never forgot what it was like to be poor.

From *Whose Tale Is True?: Readers Theatre to Introduce and Research 49 Amazing American Women* by Nancy Polette. Westport, CT: Teacher Ideas Press. Copyright © 2008.

Molly Brown No. 3: We were rich enough so that I could travel to Europe and Africa and made a lot of friends in high places. I was in Egypt in 1912 when I got word that my grandson was seriously ill. I booked passage on the *Titanic*, which promised to get me to the States in fewer than six days.

Host: Tell us about your experiences on the *Titanic*.

Molly Brown No. 1: I was in my stateroom watching television when I felt a terrible jolt. We had hit an iceberg. I heard people screaming, so I grabbed my chinchilla coat and headed for the main deck.

Molly Brown No. 2: There was such panic, and because I had never learned to read, I could not read the instructions given us about what to do in an emergency. I was so frightened. I managed to get into a lifeboat before the *Titanic* sank.

Molly Brown No. 3: The sailor in our boat did not help the frightened people, so I took charge. I got them rowing and singing to keep their spirits up. We rowed until 4:30 in the morning, when we were picked up by the ship *Carpathia*.

Host: Now it is time to decide whose tale is true. We will vote by a show of hands. Is it No. 1? Is it No. 2? Is it No. 3? Now for the moment you have all been waiting for:

Will the real Molly Brown step forward?

Answer: No. 3

No. 2 first said she could read and later said she could not.

No. 1 mentioned television, which had not yet been invented.

FURTHER READING

Blos, Joan. *Heroine of the* Titanic. Morrow, 1991,

Ruffin, Frances. *Unsinkable Molly Brown*. Powerkids Press, 2002.

REPORTING ON MARGARET TOBIN (MOLLY) BROWN

Read in the encyclopedia about Molly Brown's experience during the sinking of the *Titanic*. Complete the riddle poem by inserting the missing words.

A *Titanic* Riddle Poem

Many wanted to make the first trip

On the 1. _____, the world's largest ship.

Into the facts we now will delve.

Of this ship that sailed in 2. _____.

From Great Britain to 3. _____ _____ _____.

The passengers we all must pity.

4. _____ tons in weight

Sailing for a disaster date.

There were 5. _____ souls on board

When a 6. _____ foot gash in its side was gored.

By an 7. _____ during a lookout's lull.

It ripped and tore right through the 8. _____.

"Run for the lifeboats!" No smile and no laugh,

For the boats had room for only 9. _____.

The number of people rescued alive

Was roughly 10. _____.

The builders, they were wrong, we think,

To claim this huge ship would not sink.

Answer Key: 1-*Titanic*; 2-1912; 3-New York City; 4-46,000 tons; 5-2,200; 6-12; 7-iceberg; 8-hull; 9-half; 10-705

From *Whose Tale Is True?: Readers Theatre to Introduce and Research 49 Amazing American Women* by Nancy Polette. Westport, CT: Teacher Ideas Press. Copyright © 2008.

Mary McLeod Bethune (1875–1955)

She Started a School with $1.50

Reading Parts: Host, Mary Bethune No. 1, Mary Bethune No. 2, Mary Bethune No. 3

Host: [facing audience] Welcome to "Whose Tale Is True?" Each of our three guests claims to be the well-known educator, Mary McLeod Bethune. Only one, however, is telling the complete truth. It is up to you to decide which one is the real Mary Bethune. Now let's meet our guests. [facing readers] Welcome. Rumor has it that you started a school with only $1.50. Is this true?

Mary Bethune No. 1: I was fortunate to have a good education, and when I heard in 1904 that there was no school for young black women in Daytona Beach, Florida, I flew there to start a school with only $1.50 in my pocket.

Mary Bethune No. 2: My parents supported my desire for a good education. I worked hard in school, and in 1895 I graduated from the Moody Bible Institute, where I was the only black student. It is true that I arrived in Florida with only $1.50, but that didn't stop me from starting a school.

Mary Bethune No. 3: The school I started in Florida had five students, and the schoolhouse was a rented cottage. I sold sweet potato pies and asked for donations from church groups to keep the school going.

Host: Many schools would have welcomed you as a teacher. Why did you go to Florida to start a school when you had no money?

Mary Bethune No. 1: My parents were former slaves. I was one of 17 children, and we all had to work in the cotton fields to make a success of my parent's small farm. Fortunately I was allowed to attend the one-room schoolhouse, where I learned the value of an education. When I learned about a town where there were no schools for Negro girls, I knew it was up to me to start one.

Mary Bethune No. 2: Before I established the Daytona Literary and Industrial School for Training Negro Girls, I had the opportunity five years earlier to start a school for Negro children in Palatka, Florida, at the request of Rev. C. J. Uggans. After working five years in Palatka I felt the school was well established and I was ready for a new challenge.

Mary Bethune No. 3: Because I was an only child my parents, who were former slaves, allowed me to go to school rather than work in the fields. I was a good student at the Maysville Mission School and received scholarships to attend the Scotia Seminary and the Moody Bible Institute. After graduating I knew my life would be devoted to teaching others.

Host: In reading your biography I see that your interests went far beyond education.

Mary Bethune No. 1: Yes. I led a drive to register black voters in Daytona Beach. I was elected president of the State Federation of Colored Women's Clubs. I fought against school segregation and campaigned for better health facilities for black children.

Mary Bethune No. 2: In 1924 I became the eighth president of the National Association of Colored Women's Clubs. I helped to established the national headquarters of the clubs in Washington, D.C. My work caught the eye of those in government, and I was asked to serve on many committees and boards.

Mary Bethune No. 3: I attended the Child Welfare Conference called by President Calvin Coolidge and served on the National Commission on Child Welfare established by President Herbert Hoover. President Roosevelt appointed me director of minority affairs in the National Youth Administration. Probably the most lasting monument to my work in education, and the one of which I am most proud, is Bethune-Cookman College, which today serves the needs of young black students.

Host: Now it is time to decide whose tale is true. We will vote by a show of hands. Is it No. 1? Is it No. 2? Is it No. 3? Now for the moment you have all been waiting for:

Will the real Mary McLeod Bethune step forward?

Answer: No. 2

No. 1. mentioned flying, which was not possible in 1904.

No. 2. contradicted herself, first saying that she was one of 17 children, then that she was an only child.

FURTHER READING

Coleman, Penny. *Adventurous Women: Eight True Stories About Women Who Made a Difference*. Henry Holt, 2006.

Greenfield, Eloise. *Mary McLeod Bethune*. HarperCollins, 1994.

Jones, Amy Robin. *Mary McLeod Bethune*. Child's World, 2000

McLoone, Margo. *Mary McLeod Bethune: A Photo-Illustrated Biography*. Bridgestone Books, 1997.

ALIKE AND DIFFERENT

Mary McLeod Bethune knew that to make significant changes in the education of Negro children, the U.S. government must be involved. She served on many government committees to help bring about change. One of the first national conferences she attended was the Child Welfare Conference called by President Calvin Coolidge. It is very likely that Calvin's wife, Grace, had urged him to call such a conference. Grace Coolidge and Mary McLeod Bethune had many things in common.

Read about these two women in the encyclopedia. Put the letter G in front of any statement that applies only to Grace Coolidge. Put the letter M in front of any statement that applies only to Mary Bethune. Put the letter B in front of any statement that applies to both women.

1. _____ Before her marriage she was a teacher of the deaf.

2. _____ She raised money for a school and became one of its trustees.

3. _____ She received a gold medal from the National Institute of the Social Sciences.

4. _____ She taught at the Kendall Institute in South Carolina.

5. _____ She wanted to be a missionary in Africa.

6. _____ She believed all children should have a good education.

7. _____ She helped raise money to bring refugee children to the United States.

8. _____ When asked to give a speech, she spoke in sign language.

9. _____ She had a college education.

10. _____ She raised over $2 million for the Clarke School.

⚿ Answer Key: 1-G; 2-B; 3-G; 4-M; 5-M; 6-B; 7-G; 8-G; 9-B; 10-G

From *Whose Tale Is True?: Readers Theatre to Introduce and Research 49 Amazing American Women* by Nancy Polette. Westport, CT: Teacher Ideas Press. Copyright © 2008.

Edith Bolling Galt Wilson (1872–1961)

The First Woman "President"

Reading Parts: Host, Edith Wilson No. 1, Edith Wilson No. 2, Edith Wilson No. 3

Host: [facing audience] Welcome to "Whose Tale Is True?" Each of our three guests claims to be Edith Wilson, a first lady some called "the first woman president." Only one, however, is telling the complete truth. It is up to you to decide which one is the real Edith Wilson. Now let's meet our guests. [facing readers] Welcome. Rumor has it that you really did run the country, making important decisions for a time. Is this true?

Edith Wilson No. 1: When my husband, Woodrow Wilson, became very ill for a time during his second term in office, I did decide who should be allowed to see him and what issues should be brought to his attention. However, I made no executive decisions involving the running of the country.

Edith Wilson No. 2: I lived at a time when women were not allowed to vote. I could hardly be qualified to run the country. I came from a wealthy family that lost all their money during the Civil War. There was no money for me to have an extensive education. This is another reason I was not qualified to run the country.

Edith Wilson No. 3: I met Woodrow Wilson several months after the death of his first wife. We became very close. He often discussed national and international issues with me, both before and after we were married. I even knew the top secret code Woodrow used to send messages to Europe during World War I. If important decisions had to be made, I was qualified to make them.

Host: What kinds of decisions did you make during and after the war?

Edith Wilson No. 1: Our Constitution states that when the president cannot perform his duties, the vice president takes over. When Woodrow became ill after the war, I left all important decisions to Vice President Lyndon Johnson.

Edith Wilson No. 2: I helped the war effort by adding eight sheep to the White House lawn. The sheep kept the grass down, allowing the gardeners to do more important war work. I often decoded incoming messages for the president and advised him more than once on what his replies should be.

Edith Wilson No. 3: One real problem I had was the messages for the president that arrived at the White House from Europe in code. Only the president was able to decode them, and he was too ill. There may have been some important decisions that needed to be made that were not made during the time of his illness.

Host: How did you deal with the criticism you received during the president's illness?

Edith Wilson No. 1: I cried a lot. I only tried to do what was best for my husband's health. I didn't want him bothered with trivial issues.

Edith Wilson No. 2: The doctors felt it would be dangerous for the country if Woodrow resigned. I had to keep things together until he recovered. If that meant making executive decisions, then I gladly made them.

Edith Wilson No. 3: I really did not know what to do. People said such mean things about me that I stopped reading the papers and only let people see me if they were my friends.

Host: Now it is time to decide whose tale is true. We will vote by a show of hands. Is it No. 1? Is it No. 2? Is it No. 3? Now for the moment you have all been waiting for:

Will the real Edith Wilson step forward?

Answer: No. 2

No. 1 mentioned that Lyndon Johnson was vice president, but Johnson was not vice president until 1960, long after her husband was president.

No. 3 contradicted herself, first saying that she did and later that she did not know the White House code.

FURTHER READING

Giblin, James Cross. *Edith Wilson, the Woman Who Ran the United States*. Viking, 1992.

Harris, Bill. *The First Ladies Fact Book: The Stories of the Women of the White House from Martha Washington to Barbara Bush*. Black Dog and Leventhal, 2005.

WHAT DO YOU THINK?

Did Edith Wilson run the country during Woodrow Wilson's illness? Give reasons for your answer.

_____

_____

_____

_____

_____

_____

_____

_____

_____

_____

_____

_____

_____

_____

_____

_____

_____

_____

Bessie Coleman (1893–1926)

"Queen Bess"

Reading Parts: Host, Bessie Coleman No. 1, Bessie Coleman No. 2, Bessie Coleman No. 3

Host: [facing audience] Welcome to "Whose Tale Is True?" Each of our three guests claims to be Bessie Coleman, the world's first black female pilot. Only one, however, is telling the complete truth. It is up to you to decide which one is the real Bessie Coleman. Now let's meet our guests. [facing readers] Welcome. When did you decide you wanted to become a pilot?

Bessie Coleman No. 1: I suppose I always wanted to have wings. I was born in Atlanta, Georgia in 1893, one of 13 children. My father left us when I was seven years old, and even though my mother worked at any job she could get, times were hard. Even so, she took time to teach me to read. One day I read about flight and knew that was what I wanted to do.

Bessie Coleman No. 2: Everyone laughed at my dream. There was no money for education. My two older brothers left home to live in Chicago. They sent for me and paid my way through beauty school so that I could support myself.

Bessie Coleman No. 3: One of my clients in the salon was a newspaper editor. I told him about my dream. I told him how I had saved money for flying lessons but that no one would take me as a student simply because I was an African American woman.

Host: How did you become the first black female pilot?

Bessie Coleman No. 1: In 1902 the newspaper editor, Mr. Cullen, along with his friends, put up the money for me to travel to France, where I could be accepted for flying lessons. First I had to learn to speak and understand the French language.

Bessie Coleman No. 2: When I felt that I could speak and understand French well enough, I set sail for Europe. The year was 1920. It took seven months of lessons before I got my pilot's license. I then returned to the United States, where a newspaper story was written about me and all of a sudden I was famous.

Bessie Coleman No. 3: When I finished my training I returned to the United States. My dream was to open a flying school for men and women black pilots. To raise money I performed in air shows all over the country.

Host: Were you able to open the flying school?

Bessie Coleman No. 1: By 1923 I had enough money to buy my own airplane. What a proud day that was when I took ownership! It was a Jenny biplane and would do anything I asked it to do in the sky. Having my own plane was the first step in opening a flying school.

Bessie Coleman No. 2: My plans were put on hold when I was injured in a crash just three months after I bought the plane. I was laid up for almost two years. Then I was back to doing air shows. The folks who watched liked the daring stunts I did. They gave me a nickname, "Queen Bess."

Bessie Coleman No. 3: In 1926, when I was 40 years old, my career as a pilot ended. I was thrown out of a plane at 2,000 feet. Unfortunately I was not wearing a parachute. But I think that in my short life I inspired people of all races to not give up on their dreams.

Host: Now it is time to decide whose tale is true. We will vote by a show of hands. Is it No. 1? Is it No. 2? Is it No. 3? Now for the moment you have all been waiting for.

Will the real Bessie Coleman step forward?

Answer: No. 2

No. 1 said she took flying lessons in 1902. She would have been only 10 years old.

No. 3 said she was 40 years old in 1926. She was born in 1893, which would have made her 33 years old.

FURTHER READING

Borden, Louise. *Fly High: The Story of Bessie Coleman*. Margaret McElderry Books, 2001.

Hacker, Carlotta. *Great African-Americans in History*. Crabtree, 1997.

REPORTING ON BESSIE COLEMAN

CHEERFUL

_____
_____
_____
_____
_____

COMPETENT

_____
_____
_____
_____
_____

BESSIE COLEMAN

CALAMITY

_____
_____
_____
_____
_____

CATALYST

_____
_____
_____
_____
_____

Amelia Earhart (1897–1937)

She Opened the Skies to Women

Reading Parts: Host, Amelia Earhart No. 1, Amelia Earhart No. 2, Amelia Earhart No. 3

Host: [facing audience] Welcome to "Whose Tale Is True?" Each of our three guests claims to be Amelia Earhart, the first woman to fly across the Atlantic Ocean alone. Only one, however, is telling the complete truth. It is up to you to decide which one is the real Amelia Earhart. Now let's meet our guests. [facing readers] Welcome. When did you decide you wanted to become a pilot? Is it true that you fell in love with airplanes when you were a child?

Amelia Earhart No. 1: I was six years old when the Wright brothers made their first flight in 1903. At that time few people could see the practical value in their invention. When I was 10 years old I had a chance to see a real airplane at a country fair. I thought it was ugly.

Amelia Earhart No. 2: Yes, I was born in 1897 and fell in love with the idea of flying in a plane when I was five years old. It seemed more exciting to me than riding in Henry Ford's automobile. Even at that young age I was always ready for an adventure.

Amelia Earhart No. 3: I didn't really become interested in airplanes until I was a young adult. I was visiting in California and attended an air meet with friends. Airplane rides were being offered, and my friends dared me to take a ride. Never one to refuse a dare, I had a 10-minute ride and decided right then and there that I would become a pilot.

Host: It seems you weren't satisfied with merely learning to fly. You were out to break records and were very successful.

Amelia Earhart No. 1: That is true. I wanted to open up the skies for women. The first record I broke was the women's altitude record, taking my plane to a height of 14,000 feet. In 1928 I was the first woman to cross the Atlantic Ocean by air, not as a pilot but as a passenger.

Amelia Earhart No. 2: People laugh today at the idea of my being the first woman to fly across the Atlantic Ocean as a passenger. It is the two male pilots who should be cheered. They flew through very rough weather. Four years later I did pilot my own plane alone across the Atlantic. It took almost 15 hours.

Amelia Earhart No. 3: I broke the women's altitude record and in 1935 was the first woman to fly from the state of Hawaii to the state of California. Believe me, it was not an easy flight to make!

Host: Had you always wanted to be a pilot, or did you work in other jobs?

Amelia Earhart No. 1: I trained as a nurse and served as a military nurse in Canada during World War I.

Amelia Earhart No. 2: I got tired of nursing and spent some time as a social worker in Boston in the 1920s.

Amelia Earhart No. 3: Flying was always the love of my life. That is why I tried crossing the Pacific Ocean as part of an around-the-world flight with Fred Noonan, my navigator, in 1937. No one knows what happened to us. We were never seen again.

Host: Now it is time to decide whose tale is true. We will vote by a show of hands. Is it No. 1? Is it No. 2? Is it No. 3? Now for the moment you have all been waiting for:

Will the real Amelia Earhart step forward?

Answer: No. 1

No. 2 could not have been in love with planes in 1902, when she was five years old. The Wright brothers' first flight was in December 1903.

No. 3 mentioned the state of Hawaii in 1935. Hawaii did not become a state until 1959.

FURTHER READING

Adler, David. *Picture Book of Amelia Earhart*. Holiday House, 1998.

Anderson, Jameson. *Amelia Earhart, Legendary Aviator*. Graphic Library, 2007.

Brown, Jonathan. *Amelia Earhart*. Weekly Reader, 2005.

From *Whose Tale Is True?: Readers Theatre to Introduce and Research 49 Amazing American Women* by Nancy Polette. Westport, CT: Teacher Ideas Press. Copyright © 2008.

SPECULATION!

Challenge Question

There are many theories about what happened on Amelia Earhart's last flight. Did the plane crash in the ocean? Did she land on an island? Was she shot down or captured by the Japanese? Do you have a different theory? Complete this pattern, telling what you think happened.

What ever happened to Amelia Earhart?

Did she _____

_____

_____

_____

Or perhaps she _____

_____

_____

_____

But the best explanation for what really happened is _____

_____

_____

_____

_____

_____

_____

_____

Anna Eleanor Roosevelt (1884–1962)

Amazing First Lady

Reading Parts: Host, Eleanor Roosevelt No. 1, Eleanor Roosevelt No. 2, Eleanor Roosevelt No. 3

Host: [facing audience] Welcome to "Whose Tale Is True?" Each of our three guests claims to be Eleanor Roosevelt, first lady of the land. Only one, however, is telling the complete truth. It is up to you to decide which one is the real Eleanor Roosevelt. Now let's meet our guests. [facing readers] Welcome. Did you ever dream that you would be the first lady of the United States?

Eleanor Roosevelt No. 1: Not at all. I was a very shy child and preferred my own company to the company of others. The thought of being the center of attention as the first lady would have greatly frightened me. I never really learned the duties of a hostess.

Eleanor Roosevelt No. 2: I was an orphan by the age of eight. My family was wealthy, and I was raised by my grandmother. She was a somewhat stern woman, and although she saw to it that I was well taken care of and well educated, she showed me little affection.

Eleanor Roosevelt No. 3: When I was 15 I went to France to study. I was very good at languages and had a soft heart for anyone in need. My French teacher taught me that these were things to be proud of. She helped me to feel like a worthwhile person.

Host: I understand that 1905 was an important year for you.

Eleanor Roosevelt No. 1: I was married to Franklin Roosevelt in 1905. We had six children, and I did all I could to help Franklin climb the political ladder. He served in the New York State Senate and then became an assistant secretary of the navy. I quickly learned how to be a good hostess in Washington.

Eleanor Roosevelt No. 2: Franklin came down with polio in 1921. My job was to nurse him back to health. He never fully regained the use of his legs, so I became the one the one who traveled and kept

From *Whose Tale Is True?: Readers Theatre to Introduce and Research 49 Amazing American Women* by Nancy Polette. Westport, CT: Teacher Ideas Press. Copyright © 2008.

him informed on current affairs. In 1933 Franklin was elected president of the United States. I became the first lady.

Eleanor Roosevelt No. 3: When Franklin became president I had to keep him informed. During his second term the United States was involved in a world war. I traveled across the Atlantic and Pacific to bring aid to our fighting men and to keep Franklin informed of battlefield conditions.

Host: Your husband died just before the end of World War II. Did this mean you could retire from public life?

Eleanor Roosevelt No. 1: At first I thought I would retire to our estate at Hyde Park and take life easy. However, when I was asked to serve as the U.S. Representative to the United Nations I could not say no.

Eleanor Roosevelt No. 2: Both at home and in the United Nations I fought for human rights, racial equality, decent housing, and education for all. I was one of the authors of the *Universal Declaration of Human Rights*.

Eleanor Roosevelt No. 3: After Franklin's death I retired to our estate in Hyde Park. I did not lose contact with the world, however. I continued to send and receive e-mail until my death in 1962.

Host: Now it is time to decide whose tale is true. We will vote by a show of hands. Is it No. 1? Is it No. 2? Is it No. 3? Now for the moment you have all been waiting for:

Will the real Eleanor Roosevelt step forward?

Answer: No. 2

No. 1 contradicted herself about hostess duties.

No. 3 mentioned e-mail, which had not yet been invented.

FURTHER READING

Brown, Jonathan. *Eleanor Roosevelt*. World Almanac Library, 2002.

Rosenberg, Pam. *Eleanor Roosevelt, First Lady, Humanitarian, World Citizen*. Child's World, 2004.

From *Whose Tale Is True?: Readers Theatre to Introduce and Research 49 Amazing American Women* by Nancy Polette. Westport, CT: Teacher Ideas Press. Copyright © 2008.

REPORTING ON ELEANOR ROOSEVELT

Write an ABC report about Eleanor Roosevelt. Summarize her life and work in 26 sentences, each beginning with a letter of the alphabet from A to Z. The first two lines have been filled in for you.

A nna Eleanor Roosevelt was born in 1884.

B eing very shy, as a child she preferred her own company.

C _____

D _____

E _____

F _____

G _____

H _____

I _____

J _____

K _____

L _____

M _____

N _____

O _____

P _____

Q _____

R _____

S _____

T _____

U _____

V _____

W _____

X _____

Y _____

Z _____

Shirley Chisholm (1924–2005)

First Black Congresswoman

Reading Parts: Host, Shirley Chisholm No. 1, Shirley Chisholm No. 2, Shirley Chisholm No. 3

Host: [facing audience] Welcome to "Whose Tale Is True?" Each of our three guests claims to be Shirley Chisholm, the first African American congresswoman. Only one, however, is telling the complete truth. It is up to you to decide which one is the real Shirley Chisholm. Now let's meet our guests. [facing readers] Welcome. You were born at a time when very few women held political office. What led you to become involved in politics?

Shirley Chisholm No. 1: A good education should lead to concern about the state of one's country and what can be done to make life better for all people. I was fortunate to get a good education in the British schools on Barbados. In 1933 I returned to the United States and took great interest in watching politicians on television.

Shirley Chisholm No. 2: My mother was born in Barbados. I was born in Brooklyn in 1924, but making a decent living was difficult for black people in the 1920s, so my parents sent me to live with my grandmother in Barbados, where I went to school and learned about the importance of government. I was nine years old when I returned to the United States and I greatly admired the new president, Theodore Roosevelt.

Shirley Chisholm No. 3: I was first exposed to politics as a student at Brooklyn College. I formed a club for black students and after college started the Unity Democratic Club to mobilize black people to register and vote and to have a voice in their government.

Host: How did your college education help you politically?

Shirley Chisholm No. 1: I majored in sociology and education and learned the value of speaking out on issues of the day. I wanted the poor people of the United States to have better lives and was never afraid to voice my opinion, backed up with facts.

90 From *Whose Tale Is True?: Readers Theatre to Introduce and Research 49 Amazing American Women* by Nancy Polette. Westport, CT: Teacher Ideas Press. Copyright © 2008.

Shirley Chisholm No. 2: I got a degree in education but found it difficult to get a job after college. I taught at a nursery school and at the same time set up day care centers for working mothers. These were so successful that my name became well known in Brooklyn and I was elected to the New York State Legislature.

Shirley Chisholm No. 3: I was an outspoken legislator, and people must have liked what I had to say. After four years in the New York Legislature I was elected to the U.S. Congress, where I served seven terms, from 1968 to 1982.

Host: I understand that you were the first woman to run for president of the United States.

Shirley Chisholm No. 1: That is not true. I was not the first woman to run for president of the United States. Victoria Woodhull has that honor. She ran for president in 1872.

Shirley Chisholm No. 2: In 1972 I campaigned to win the Democratic Party nomination. As president I would be in a better position to reach my goal of equality for all.

Shirley Chisholm No. 3: In 1972 I decided to run for president of the United States. During my time in Congress I had an all-female office staff and spoke out strongly for civil rights, women's rights, and against the Vietnam War. My campaign slogan was "Fighting Shirley Chisholm, Unbought and Unbossed!"

Host: Now it is time to decide whose tale is true. We will vote by a show of hands. Is it No. 1? Is it No. 2? Is it No. 3? Now for the moment you have all been waiting for:

Will the real Shirley Chisholm step forward?

Answer: No. 3

No. 1 mentioned television, which was not available in 1933.

No. 2 named the wrong president. In 1933 the president was Franklin D. Roosevelt, not Theodore Roosevelt.

FURTHER READING

Pollack, Jill S. *Shirley Chisholm*. Franklin Watts, 1994.

Schraeder, Catherine. *Shirley Chisholm, Teacher and Congresswoman*. Enslow, 1990.

SLOGANS

Shirley Chisholm's campaign slogan was: "Fighting Shirley Chisholm, Unbought and Unbossed!" Here are more campaign slogans:

Campaign	Candidate	Slogan
1900	William McKinley	A full dinner pail
1916	Woodrow Wilson	He kept us out of war
1952	Dwight Eisenhower	I like Ike
1976	Gerald Ford	He's making us proud again
1976	Jimmy Carter	Not just peanuts
1984	Ronald Reagan	It's morning again in America
1988	George Bush	Kinder, gentler nation
2000	George W. Bush	Leave no child behind

If you were to run for president today, what would be your campaign slogan? Design a poster that features your slogan. The slogan should tell the voters about an issue you feel is important.

Leontyne Price (1927–   )

Operas Were Written for Her

Reading Parts: Host, Leontyne Price No. 1, Leontyne Price No. 2, Leontyne Price No. 3

Host: [facing audience] Welcome to "Whose Tale Is True?" Each of our three guests claims to be Leontyne Price, world famous opera star. Only one, however, is telling the complete truth. It is up to you to decide which one is the real Leontyne Price. Now let's meet our guests. [facing readers] Welcome. How amazing it is that a little girl born of working-class parents in Mississippi became an opera star acclaimed all over the world. Tell us how this happened.

Leontyne Price No. 1: I began my musical education at a very early age. My mother had a beautiful voice and was my inspiration as a singer.

Leontyne Price No. 2: I began singing in public at age three and started piano lessons at age five. I liked people wanting to hear me play and decided by age six that I would be a performer.

Leontyne Price No. 3: My mother took me to hear a concert by Marian Anderson. She looked so beautiful on the stage and her voice was so thrilling that I decided then and there that I would be a performer, too.

Host: Tell us how your musical career developed.

Leontyne Price No. 1: In high school I was the pianist for musical shows and sang in the chorus. I never had a chance to play leading parts in the musicals.

Leontyne Price No. 2: After high school I was a music education major at Central State University in Ohio. After hearing me sing, the college president told me to major in voice, and I won a full tuition scholarship to the Julliard School in New York.

Leontyne Price No. 3: I received a scholarship to the Julliard School in New York, where a producer saw me in a student production and, in 1954, offered me a leading role in his opera, *Four Saints in*

From *Whose Tale Is True?: Readers Theatre to Introduce and Research 49 Amazing American Women* by Nancy Polette. Westport, CT: Teacher Ideas Press. Copyright © 2008.

Three Acts. I immediately e-mailed him my acceptance and played the starring role on Broadway for three weeks.

Host: How did you move from this first starring role to singing all over the world?

Leontyne Price No. 1: From playing leading parts in high school musicals to that first role on Broadway, in 1954 I starred as Bess in George Gershwin's *Porgy and Bess*. The show was such a success that we toured the world with it.

Leontyne Price No. 2: After my success in 1954 I was offered many roles and sang in recital halls, on opera stages, and on television. In 1960 I was the first black singer to sing a major role at the famed La Scala Opera House.

Leontyne Price No. 3: From 1954 to 1977 I sang many different roles in opera houses all over the world. I won 18 Grammy Awards and in 1964 was awarded the Presidential Freedom Award.

Host: Now it is time to decide whose tale is true. We will vote by a show of hands. Is it No. 1? Is it No. 2? Is it No. 3? Now for the moment you have all been waiting for:

Will the real Leontyne Price step forward?

Answer: No. 2

No. 1 contradicted herself, saying first that she did not and then that she did star in high school musicals.

No. 3 mentioned e-mail, which was not available in 1954.

FURTHER READING

Bolden, Tanya. *Not Afraid to Dare*. Scholastic, 1998.

Williams, Sylvia B. *Leontyne Price, Opera Superstar*. Children's Press, 1984.

TAKE A POLL

Leontyne Price's favorite instrument was the piano. Ask 10 people at school or at home which of the musical instruments in the following chart is their favorite. The instrument with the most Xs under its name is the winner.

Person's Name	drum	guitar	piano	flute	trumpet	organ
1.						
2.						
3.						
4.						
5.						
6.						
7.						
8.						
9.						
10.						

A. The favorite instrument of boys was the _____

B. The favorite instrument of girls was the _____

C. The instrument with the most votes from everyone was _____

Margaret Bourke-White (1906–1971)

She Photographed the World

Reading Parts: Host, Margaret Bourke-White No. 1, Margaret Bourke-White No. 2, Margaret Bourke-White No. 3

Host: [facing audience] Welcome to "Whose Tale Is True?" Each of our three guests claims to be Margaret Bourke-White, who photographed the world. Only one, however, is telling the complete truth. It is up to you to decide which one is the real Margaret Bourke-White. Now let's meet our guests. [facing readers] Welcome. We know that you are famous for telling news stories in pictures. How did you get interested in photography?

Margaret Bourke-White No. 1: I was certainly not a young camera buff. My father loved all of the outdoors and often took me on nature walks. From him I learned to see the world in a different way. I thought snakes were among the most beautiful creatures on Earth.

Margaret Bourke-White No. 2: One day I found a puff adder and was so thrilled that I took it to school. I wore it wrapped around my neck like a scarf. The teacher wasn't thrilled. She sent me home.

Margaret Bourke-White No. 3: When I entered Cornell University I planned on being a herpetologist and spend my life studying birds. Then I took a photography course that changed my mind. I could share the world I saw with others through the camera.

Host: How did you move from your love of photography to becoming a world famous photographer?

Margaret Bourke-White No. 1: I opened my own studio and ventured to photograph images never before seen, like the fiery furnaces of the steel mill. Henry Luce of *Fortune Magazine* saw my photographs and hired me in 1929.

From *Whose Tale Is True?: Readers Theatre to Introduce and Research 49 Amazing American Women* by Nancy Polette. Westport, CT: Teacher Ideas Press. Copyright © 2008.

Margaret Bourke-White No. 2: The assignments I was given at *Fortune Magazine* ranged from photographing slaughterhouses to a day in the life of Joseph Stalin. I had to travel to Poland to get the Stalin photos. In the 1930s I was hired by *Life Magazine*. One of my photos was on the first cover of *Life*.

Margaret Bourke-White No. 3: I had many assignments for *Life Magazine*. I photographed the poverty of the South. When World War II broke out I was one of the very few women war correspondents.

Host: Was your life in danger while photographing the war in Europe?

Margaret Bourke-White No. 1: I took photos of soldiers and war victims and was often on the front lines. I photographed the starving prisoners liberated from the concentration camps. It was the most difficult assignment of all.

Margaret Bourke-White No. 2: I spent hours on a hotel roof in Moscow photographing German air raids while all the other guests took shelter in the basement.

Margaret Bourke-White No. 3: A ship I was on was torpedoed, and I photographed the sinking ship from a lifeboat.

Host: Now it is time to decide whose tale is true. We will vote by a show of hands. Is it No. 1? Is it No. 2? Is it No. 3? Now for the moment you have all been waiting for:

Will the real Margaret Bourke-White step forward?

Answer: No. 1

No. 2 said she photographed Stalin in Poland. He was Russian.

No. 3 said a herpetologist studies birds. A herpetologist studies snakes.

FURTHER READING

Daffron, Carolyn. *Margaret Bourke-White*. Chelsea House, 1988.

Rubin, Susan. *Margaret Bourke-White: Her Pictures Were Her Life*. Abrams, 1999.

From *Whose Tale Is True?: Readers Theatre to Introduce and Research 49 Amazing American Women* by Nancy Polette. Westport, CT: Teacher Ideas Press. Copyright © 2008.

REPORTING ON MARGARET BOURKE-WHITE

Follow the pattern below to write an "Only One" report about Margaret Bourke-White
The first two are done for you. How many can you add?

There were many children born in 1906 but ONLY ONE became a world famous woman photographer.
There were many snakes in the woods but ONLY ONE was worn as a scarf by Margaret Bourke-White.

There were many _____
_____

But only one _____
_____

There were many _____
_____

But only one _____
_____

There were many _____
_____

But only one _____
_____

There were many _____
_____

But only one _____
_____

There were many _____
_____

But only one _____
_____

There were many _____
_____

But only one _____
_____

From *Whose Tale Is True?: Readers Theatre to Introduce and Research 49 Amazing American Women* by Nancy Polette. Westport, CT: Teacher Ideas Press. Copyright © 2008.

Jacqueline Cochran (1910–1980)

Record Breaker in the Sky

Reading Parts: Host, Jacqueline Cochran No. 1, Jacqueline Cochran No. 2, Jacqueline Cochran No. 3

Host: [facing audience] Welcome to "Whose Tale Is True?" Each of our three guests claims to be Jacqueline Cochran, who broke world aviation records. Only one, however, is telling the complete truth. It is up to you to decide which one is the real Jacqueline Cochran. Now let's meet our guests. [facing readers] Welcome. We know that you are a very famous aviator who grew up in Florida. Did you take flying lessons at an early age?

Jacqueline Cochran No. 1: I was only 10 years old when people started seeing planes in the air. These were the barnstormers that went from one town to another to put on air shows. My family was so poor that buying an air show ticket was the last thing my father would have done.

Jacqueline Cochran No. 2: As a teen, planes were the farthest thing from my mind. I had to earn my own living, so I went to work in a beauty shop. My dream was to develop a line of cosmetics and some day own my own company even though I never finished high school.

Jacqueline Cochran No. 3: In 1929 I got a job at Saks Beauty Salon in New York City. Sometimes I traveled with wealthy customers. I met and married Floyd Odlum, who was a millionaire. He helped me achieve my dream of owning my own cosmetics business.

Host: It seems a long way from making cosmetics to breaking world aviation records. How did you get interested in flying?

Jacqueline Cochran No. 1: My husband suggested that a business that covered the entire country would mean a lot of travel for me. He suggested I take flying lessons. I earned my pilot's license in three weeks and have been flying ever since.

Jacqueline Cochran No. 2: I entered my first flight competition in 1934 and another in 1935. I had to drop out both times because of mechanical problems. I was not discouraged. Two years later I won several races and set new air speed records from New York to Miami. Pretty good, I think, for a high school graduate.

Jacqueline Cochran No. 3: In 1938 I won the Bendix cross-country race. I was determined to break even more world records, but then World War II broke out.

Host: What was your role in World War II?

Jacqueline Cochran No. 1: In 1951, during World War II, I piloted a bomber to England, and as a flight captain for the British Air Force I trained women pilots for air transport service.

Jacqueline Cochran No. 2: Two years later I became director of the Women's Air Force Service. We trained more than 1,000 women pilots to transport planes from factories to air bases and wherever else they were needed.

Jacqueline Cochran No. 3: After the war I continued to set records. I was the first woman to break the sound barrier in a jet and set both speed and altitude records as a test pilot.

Host: Now it is time to decide whose tale is true. We will vote by a show of hands. Is it No. 1? Is it No. 2? Is it No. 3? Now for the moment you have all been waiting for:

Will the real Jacqueline Cochran step forward?

Answer: No. 3

No. 1 said World War II took place in 1951; it ended in 1945.

No. 2 contradicted herself about graduating from high school.

FURTHER READING

Smith, Elizabeth. *Coming Out Rght: The Story of Jacqueline Cochran.* Walker, 1991.

REPORTING ON JACQUELINE COCHRAN

Use information from the "Whose Tale Is True" script to write four questions and one answer about Jacqueline Cochran.

HOW did Jacqueline Cochran become a world famous aviator?

DID SHE _____

_____?

MAYBE SHE _____

_____?

OR COULD IT BE THAT SHE _____

_____?

WAS THERE _____

_____?

MY BEST GUESS IS _____

_____.

Virginia Hall (1906–1982)

Master Spy

Reading Parts: Host, Virginia Hall No. 1, Virginia Hall No. 2, Virginia Hall No. 3

Host: [facing audience] Welcome to "Whose Tale Is True?" Each of our three guests claims to be Virginia Hall, one of the nation's most effective spies in World War II. Only one, however, is telling the complete truth. It is up to you to decide which one is the real Virginia Hall. Now let's meet our guests. [facing readers] Welcome. Was it always your ambition to serve your country as a master spy?

Virginia Hall No. 1: Not at all. As a child I spent summers at our family farm and spent many days roaming the woods and finding injured animals. I set up an animal hospital in the barn, It was my first step toward becoming a veterinarian.

Virginia Hall No. 2: My ambition was to travel the world as a woman diplomat. I studied many languages and learned to speak French, Italian, German, and some Russian fairly well.

Virginia Hall No. 3: My father liked to travel and took the whole family with him. At the drop of a hat we would be jetting off to Spain or Italy or Switzerland or some other place. I knew from these travels that I wanted to spend my life traveling. What better way to do it than as a woman diplomat?

Host: How did your dream of becoming the first woman diplomat die, and how did your role as a spy begin?

Virginia Hall No. 1: After college I got a job as a clerk with the diplomatic service overseas. I lost my leg in a hunting accident in 1931. It was replaced with a computer-operated leg. Diplomats, I was told, could not have an artificial leg.

Virginia Hall No. 2: I left the diplomatic service after the hunting accident and was in Paris when the Germans invaded France. I traveled to England, where the British spy agency, the OSS, asked me to go back to France as a spy. I agreed and received special training.

Virginia Hall No. 3: In France I disguised myself as a milkmaid and reported German troop movements and the location of good landing fields or supplies on my radio each night. I had to move frequently because the Germans would bomb any house suspected of having a radio.

Host: Were you ever captured by the Germans, and did the United States ever recognize how valuable your work as an allied agent was?

Virginia Hall No. 1: The Germans issued a bulletin saying that I was one of the most dangerous Allied agents in France and must be destroyed. I escaped by making a 54-hour climb across the mountains into Spain.

Virginia Hall No. 2: I stayed in Spain a short time but then returned to southern France, where I was not so well known. After D-Day I told the Allied armies where to find the retreating Germans. The Frenchmen I worked with captured 500 German soldiers and held them until the Allied armies arrived.

Virginia Hall No. 3: I was the only civilian in World War II to receive the nation's second highest honor, the Distinguished Service Cross. I felt I didn't deserve it. After all, I only did my job.

Host: Now it is time to decide whose tale is true. We will vote by a show of hands. Is it No. 1? Is it No. 2? Is it No. 3? Now for the moment you have all been waiting for:

Will the real Virginia Hall step forward?

Answer: No. 2

No. 1 talked about a computerized artificial leg. There were no computers in World War II.

No. 3 talked about "jetting" off to foreign lands. There were no jets when she was a child.

FURTHER READING

Binney, Marcus. *The Women Who Lived for Danger*. William Morrow, 2003.

McIntosh, Elizabeth. *Sisterhood of Spies: The Women of the OSS*. Dell Publishing, Random House, 1998.

CHECK THESE OUT!

American history reveals many women spies who showed great courage in serving their country in time of war.

Match the spy with the war in which she was involved by placing the number of the war in front of the woman's name.

Find information about three of these spies. Choose one for an award. What will the award be for?

1. Revolutionary War   2. Civil War

A. _____ Lydia Darragh

B. _____ Belle Boyd

C. _____ Nancy Hart

D. _____ Antonia Ford

E. _____ Sybil Luddington

F. _____ Rose Greenhow

G. _____ Mary Elizabeth Bowser

H. _____ Ginny Moon

I. _____ Emily Geiger

J. _____ Elizabeth Van Lew

K. _____ Mary Touvestre

Name _____

is to be awarded the Medal of _____

for her role in _____

_____

Answer Key: A-1; B-2; C-2; D-2; E-1; F-2; G-2; H-2; I-2; J-2; K-2

Marian Anderson (1897–1993)

"A Voice Such As One Hears Once in a Hundred Years"

Reading Parts: Host, Marian Anderson No. 1, Marian Anderson No. 2, Marian Anderson No. 3

Host: [facing audience] Welcome to "Whose Tale Is True?" Each of our three guests claims to be one of the greatest singers the world has ever known. Only one, however, is telling the complete truth. It is up to you to decide which one is the real Marian Anderson. Now let's meet our guests. [facing readers] Welcome. As a child, did you dream of singing for kings and queens of Europe?

Marian Anderson No. 1: Absolutely not. My family was poor, and as a child I cleaned houses to earn money we needed for food. I loved singing and sang as I cleaned. Even as an eight-year-old I was told that my voice was special.

Marian Anderson No. 2: I looked forward to Sundays, when I sang in the church choir. As I got older, more and more people came to the church concerts. Church members donated money so that I could have voice lessons.

Marian Anderson No. 3: Even though I could pay for the lessons, the local music school would not take me as a pupil. The admissions clerk told me they did not admit Negroes. I did find a teacher who gave me lessons for free.

Host: Tell us about your first recital at New York's Town Hall.

Marian Anderson No. 1: I was not well received. I had had a difficult time learning the foreign languages in which the songs needed to be sung. The critics were not kind. I almost gave up singing, but my mother convinced me to keep on with my studies and concerts.

Marian Anderson No. 2: That first Town Hall concert was not very successful. I tripped over some of the foreign words in the songs, and as an African American singer I was not well received.

From *Whose Tale Is True?: Readers Theatre to Introduce and Research 49 Amazing American Women* by Nancy Polette. Westport, CT: Teacher Ideas Press. Copyright © 2008.

Marian Anderson No. 3: For four years before the Town Hall concert in 1924 I had toured the United States giving concerts. I was well received by African American audiences but not by others. I decided to continue my studies in London.

Host: We know that you achieved great success in both Europe and the United States. How did this come about?

Marian Anderson No. 1: After the 1924 Town Hall concert I was ready to stop singing, but my voice teacher insisted that I continue my studies in London. For the next 10 years I was a great success throughout Europe and returned to the United States to become the first African American to sing at the Metropolitan Opera.

Marian Anderson No. 2: My concerts were well received in Europe from 1925 until 1945, when I returned to the United States. The Easter Sunday concert I gave on the steps of the Lincoln Memorial in 1939 was attended by 75,000 people.

Marian Anderson No. 3: After great success as a singer in Europe. I gave many concerts in the United States. I sang at the inaugurations of Presidents Dwight Eisenhower and John Kennedy and received the Presidential Medal of Freedom from President Lyndon Johnson.

Host: Now it is time to decide whose tale is true. We will vote by a show of hands. Is it No. 1? Is it No. 2? Is it No. 3? Now for the moment you have all been waiting for:

Will the real Marian Anderson step forward?

Answer: No. 3

No. 1 first said her mother urged her to continue her career, then said it was her teacher who did that.

No. 2 said she returned to the United States in 1945 but gave a concert at the Lincoln memorial in 1939.

FURTHER READING

Freedman, Russell. *The Voice That Challenged a Nation.* Clarion Books, 2004.

McKissack, Patricia. *Marian Anderson, Great Singer.* Enslow, 2001.

Ryan, Pam. *When Marian Sang.* Scholastic, 2002.

CREATE A MARIAN ANDERSON DATA BANK: WRITE A REPORT

Early Life	Youth	What Others Say
_____	_____	_____
_____	_____	_____
_____	_____	_____
_____	_____	_____
_____	_____	_____
_____	_____	_____
_____	_____	_____
_____	_____	_____

Dreams	Difficulties	Accomplishments
_____	_____	_____
_____	_____	_____
_____	_____	_____
_____	_____	_____
_____	_____	_____
_____	_____	_____
_____	_____	_____
_____	_____	_____

WRITE YOUR REPORT. Include:

1. A beginning that "hooks" the reader.
2. Tell WHO, WHEN, and WHERE.
3. Tell what others say about the person.
4. Show difficulties that were overcome.
5. Use action sentences to tell what he/she did.
6. Tell about his/her accomplishments.
7. End by referring to the beginning or asking a question.

From *Whose Tale Is True?: Readers Theatre to Introduce and Research 49 Amazing American Women* by Nancy Polette. Westport, CT: Teacher Ideas Press. Copyright © 2008.

Anna Mary Robertson (Grandma Moses) (1860–1961)

Her Paintings Preserved a Way of Life

Reading Parts: Host, Grandma Moses No. 1, Grandma Moses No. 2, Grandma Moses No. 3

Host: [facing audience] Welcome to "Whose Tale Is True?" Each of our three guests claims to be Grandma Moses, American folk artist. Only one, however, is telling the complete truth. It is up to you to decide which one is the real Grandma Moses. Now let's meet our guests. [facing readers] Welcome. Your biography says that you were born in 1860. Did you show artistic talent as a child?

Grandma Moses No. 1: Yes I did, which was unusual for a farm girl in the 1860s. My folks recognized my talent and scraped together what little money they could so I could have art lessons.

Grandma Moses No. 2: Growing up on a farm in the 1860s meant everybody worked from dawn to dusk. We ate what the land provided and every child had chores from the youngest to the oldest. There was no time for foolishness like art.

Grandma Moses No. 3: I grew up on a farm in upstate New York and married Thomas Moses in 1865. As a farmer's wife with five children to raise, there was no time for painting pictures. I did, however, make embroidery pictures when evening came and the day's chores were done.

Host: What led you to painting pictures?

Grandma Moses No. 1: As a teenager I got a scholarship to art school, and that is where I learned to paint. Thomas Gainsborough, who did that *Pinky* picture, was my favorite instructor.

Grandma Moses No. 2: By the time I was my seventies the arthritis in my hands was so bad that I switched from embroidery to painting. I never had an art lesson. I just painted the people and places I grew up with. Folks liked my pictures, and I sold a few at the local fairs along with my canned preserves.

From *Whose Tale Is True?: Readers Theatre to Introduce and Research 49 Amazing American Women* by Nancy Polette. Westport, CT: Teacher Ideas Press. Copyright © 2008.

Grandma Moses No. 3: By the time I was 80 years old I had painted a few pictures and given some to friends, who seemed to like them. Then a fellow from a New York art gallery saw some of my pictures in the local drug store window and told me he wanted lots more. In the next 20 years I painted over 1,600 pictures.

Host: Your name became a household word all over the United States. How did that happen?

Grandma Moses No. 1: In 1938 Gimbel's department store displayed my paintings. Eleven years later President Harry Truman presented me with an award for outstanding accomplishment in art.

Grandma Moses No. 2: The Hallmark people wanted to use some of my paintings on their greeting cards, so folks everywhere knew a Grandma Moses painting when they saw one. More folks saw my work when I was on a television program with Edward R. Murrow in 1951. I was 91 years old at the time.

Grandma Moses No. 3: I reckon if you paint enough pictures, some folks are bound to see one or the other. I painted over 1,600 pictures, and at age 100 I illustrated Clement Moore's *Night Before Christmas*. I guess I showed that old folks can be as useful and as productive as young people.

Host: Now it is time to decide whose tale is true. We will vote by a show of hands. Is it No. 1? Is it No. 2? Is it No. 3? Now for the moment you have all been waiting for:

Will the real Grandma Moses step forward?

Answer: No. 2

No. 1 could not have had Gainsborough as a teacher. He died in 1788.

No. 3 said she married in 1865. She was born in 1860, which means she would have married at age five.

FURTHER READING

Schaefer, Adam. *Grandma Moses.* Heinemann, 2003.

Wallner, Alexandra. *Grandma Moses.* Holiday House, 2004.

DESCRIPTIVE COMPARISONS

1. Read one of the short biographies of Grandma Moses listed on the previous page or an encyclopedia or Internet article about her. On the lines list adjectives that describe her personality, special qualities, and talents.

generous _____ _____ _____

_____ _____ _____ _____

_____ _____ _____ _____

_____ _____ _____ _____

_____ _____ _____ _____

2. Now use these words to write five descriptive sentences about Grandma Moses. Each sentence must contain a simile: a comparison using the words *like* or *as*.

Example:

Grandmas Moses was as **generous** with her paintings as a Christmas Santa Claus.

Note: Grandma Moses and Santa Claus are not alike except in one way. Both give to others. Grandma gave away many of her paintings.

3. Write your similes here.

_____

_____

_____

_____

_____

From *Whose Tale Is True?: Readers Theatre to Introduce and Research 49 Amazing American Women* by Nancy Polette. Westport, CT: Teacher Ideas Press. Copyright © 2008.

Rosa Parks (1913–2005)

Mother of the Civil Rights Movement

Reading Parts: Host, Rosa Parks No. 1, Rosa Parks No. 2, Rosa Parks No. 3

Host: [facing audience] Welcome to "Whose Tale Is True?" Each of our three guests claims to be Rosa Parks, often called the mother of the civil rights movement. Only one, however, is telling the complete truth. It is up to you to decide which one is the real Rosa Parks. Now let's meet our guests. [facing readers] Welcome. How do you feel about your well-deserved title?

Rosa Parks No. 1: There are many others who deserve the title. When I refused to give up my bus seat on December 1, 1955, I had just had enough of all the injustices done to Africa Americans in Montgomery, Mississippi, and cities in other states.

Rosa Parks No. 2: I never intended to be a leader in the civil rights movement. Growing up I didn't know what "civil rights" were. Many nights I wanted to be invisible when I heard the Klan ride by and knew they were out lynching and burning down houses.

Rosa Parks No. 3: As a young woman I attended the Alabama State Teachers' College and then taught school. I married, and my husband and I joined the National Association for the Advancement of Colored People. We did what little we could to end the injustices that were part of every African American's life.

Host: Tell us about that fateful day in December 1955.

Rosa Parks No. 1: I was riding on a bus and was asked to give up my seat to a white rider. I refused even though I knew what the Alabama law said.

Rosa Parks No. 2: When the driver asked me if I was going to stand up, I told him NO. I was taken before a judge, convicted, and fined. I refused to pay the fine.

Rosa Parks No. 3: It may have seemed a strange thing to do, but I wanted to get public opinion on our side. For too long blacks had been treated as second-class citizens. It was time to challenge an unfair segregation law in the courts.

Host: How did this action influence the civil rights movement?

Rosa Parks No. 1: For the first time African Americans banded together to boycott the busses. The bus company depended on our fares getting to and from work. If there were no riders, there were no fares. We nearly put the bus company out of business.

Rosa Parks No. 2: After I paid the fine under protest, the Montgomery Improvement Association was founded to help support my case. Its leader was Dr. Martin Luther King Jr. He led the bus boycott, which lasted 382 days, a very long time for folks to go without needed transportation.

Rosa Parks No. 3: It was also a very long time for the bus company to be without our fares! The case was taken all the way to the Supreme Court, and I have a feeling the bus company was as happy as we were when the Supreme Court ruled that public transportation was for everyone and segregation was outlawed.

Host: Now it is time to decide whose tale is true. We will vote by a show of hands. Is it No. 1? Is it No. 2? Is it No. 3? Now for the moment you have all been waiting for:

Will the real Rosa Parks step forward?

Answer: No. 3

No. I stated that Montgomery is in Mississippi. The Montgomery where Rosa Parks refused to give up her bus seat is in Alabama.

No. 2 contradicted herself, first saying she did not pay the fine, then saying she did pay the fine.

FURTHER READING

Nobleman, Marc T. *Rosa Parks*. World Almanac, 2002.

Wheeler, Jill. *Rosa Parks*. Abdo & Daughters, 2003.

REPORTING ON ROSA PARKS

Fill in the blanks in this story to write a fictionalized account of what you think Rosa Parks's bus ride might have been like

THE BUS RIDE

Come with me on the bus ride to _____.

Notice the woman sitting _____.

Listen for the _____.

Follow the _____ as he approaches _____

and says "_____."

Watch the other riders as they _____

_____ and _____.

Be overwhelmed with a feeling of _____

when _____

and salute Rosa Parks, a woman brave enough to defy unjust laws.

Dolores Huerta (1930–   )

Champion of Workers' Rights

Reading Parts: Host, Dolores Huerta No. 1, Dolores Huerta No. 2, Dolores Huerta No. 3

Host: [facing audience] Welcome to "Whose Tale Is True?" Each of our three guests claims to be Dolores Huerta, champion for workers' rights. Only one, however, is telling the complete truth. It is up to you to decide which one is the real Dolores Huerta. Now let's meet our guests. [facing readers] Welcome. All of your adult life you have fought for better working conditions for farm workers. What led you in this direction?

Dolores Huerta No. 1: I was born at the beginning of the Great Depression in 1930. My father was a farm worker, and our family moved from place to place, following the harvests. Conditions were bad. Many places we lived weren't fit for human beings.

Dolores Huerta No. 2: My father was both a miner and a farm worker. Life was hard during the Depression, and my parents divorced. My mother took my two brothers and me to California, where she worked at two jobs to support us.

Dolores Huerta No. 3: Life was very hard for many people in the 1930s. My mother remarried in the 1940s and things got better. She owned a restaurant and a hotel, and I often saw her giving out free meals to hungry people.

Host: Even though your parents were divorced, wasn't it your father who inspired you to fight for farm workers?

Dolores Huerta No. 1: Yes. My father was unhappy with the working conditions of migrant workers. He got a college degree, became active in labor unions, and was elected to the New Mexico State Legislature, where he could do something about passing laws to help them. Next to my father, another man who inspired me was Cesar Chavez. I never met him, but I admired his efforts for the farm workers.

Dolores Huerta No. 2: My father's example inspired me to get a college education. I graduated and became a teacher. It broke my heart to see the children of migrant workers come to school hungry and with no shoes. I knew I had to do what I could to help.

Dolores Huerta No. 3: As I saw my father fight for better living conditions for migrant workers, I joined with Cesar Chavez to found the National Farm Workers Association. Conditions were terrible. Workers were not paid fairly for the work they did. Some were even charged for a drink of water after working hours in the hot sun. Many of us who fought for the workers were physically attacked Fortunately I was not.

Host: Were your efforts successful?

Dolores Huerta No. 1: Cesar Chavez and I convinced the grape workers to strike and led a boycott of grapes throughout the nation. The strike worked. The farm owners had a choice of paying better wages or watching their grapes rot on the vine.

Dolores Huerta No. 2: I worked with the union, held citizenship classes for the farm workers and their families, and campaigned in the California Legislature to get laws passed. It was a great day for all of us when the governor signed the Agricultural Labor Relations Act in 1975.

Dolores Huerta No. 3: I believe I have helped the farm workers. I have spoken out loudly against the injustices the workers have endured. I have negotiated contracts and lobbied government leaders for fair laws for the workers. At one peaceful demonstration I was clubbed and ended up in the hospital, but nothing will stop me from continuing the fight for justice.

Host: Now it is time to decide whose tale is true. We will vote by a show of hands. Is it No. 1? Is it No. 2? Is it No. 3? Now for the moment you have all been waiting for:

Will the real Dolores Huerta step forward?

Answer: No. 2

No. 1 contradicted herself, first saying she never met Cesar Chavez, but later saying that she worked with him.

No. 3 contradicted herself, first saying she had never been injured while fighting for the workers, then later saying she was clubbed during a peaceful demonstration.

FURTHER READING

Bowdish, Lynea. *With Courage: Seven Women Who Changed America.* Mondo, 2004.

De Ruiz, Dana Catherine, and Richard Larios. *La Causa: The Migrant Farm Workers' Story.* Raintree-Steck-Vaughn, 1992.

REPORTING ON DOLORES HUERTA

AN EIGHT-SENTENCE BIOGRAPHY REPORT

Here is an easy way to do a biography report. Follow the directions to write a biography report about Dolores Huerta.

1. Ask your reader a question about Dolores Huerta.

_____

_____

2. Name her. Tell when and where she was born and grew up.

_____

_____

3. Write an action sentence telling one thing she did as a child.

_____

_____

4. Write an action a sentence telling one thing she did as an adult.

_____

_____

5. Write a sentence about her that contains the word "because."

_____

_____

6. Tell in one sentence what others might say about her.

_____

_____

7. Tell in one sentence a problem or difficulty she faced.

_____

_____

8. Describe one of her major accomplishments.

_____

_____

From _Whose Tale Is True?: Readers Theatre to Introduce and Research 49 Amazing American Women_ by Nancy Polette. Westport, CT: Teacher Ideas Press. Copyright © 2008.

Jacqueline Kennedy Onassis (1929–1994)

She Restored the White House

Reading Parts: Host, Jacqueline Kennedy No. 1, Jacqueline Kennedy No. 2, Jacqueline Kennedy No. 3

Host: [facing audience] Welcome to "Whose Tale Is True?" Each of our three guests claims to be Jacqueline Kennedy, the first lady who gave the White House a new look. Only one, however, is telling the complete truth. It is up to you to decide which one is the real Jacqueline Kennedy. Now let's meet our guests. [facing readers] Welcome! I understand that you undertook the job of redecorating the White House to reflect the lives of its former occupants.

Jacqueline Kennedy No. 1: That is true. When we moved into the White House in 1944, the furnishings were a hodgepodge of odds and ends. Nothing matched, and no one knew which furnishings had belonged to which presidents and their families.

Jacqueline Kennedy No. 2: Each room in the White House had many beautiful things, but none of them matched, and no one knew where they had come from. I began studying files from the Library of Congress to try to identify each piece of furniture. In the attic I even found the giant, oversized bathtub used by President William McKinley after he got stuck in the standard White House tub.

Jacqueline Kennedy No. 3: I not only searched the Library of Congress files, I also searched the attic for pieces that had been stored away for years. My goal was that "everything in the White House should have a reason for being there."

Host: Did you study interior decorating in school, or before you married did you work for an interior decorator?

Jacqueline Kennedy No. 1: Far from it. I did go to Vassar for two years, but was much better at skiing, swimming, and horseback riding than interior decorating.

Jacqueline Kennedy No. 2: I had no formal training in interior decoration but have always been known for my sense of style. Some of my fashionable looks were copied and became Jackie dolls. I have always

From *Whose Tale Is True?: Readers Theatre to Introduce and Research 49 Amazing American Women* by Nancy Polette. Westport, CT: Teacher Ideas Press. Copyright © 2008.

been a reader, and old photographs and descriptions in the Library of Congress files helped me to achieve an accurate restoration of the White House.

Jacqueline Kennedy No. 3: I have had no formal training or experience in interior decorating. My first job after college was as a roving reporter for the *Washington Times Herald.* I approached strangers on the street and asked them questions while taking their pictures. My title was "Inquiring Camera Girl."

Host: What were some of the most interesting items you found and used in the restoration?

Jacqueline Kennedy No. 1: If it had not been for Caroline Harrison, who gathered and displayed pieces of china used by former first ladies, I would not have been able to complete the displays in the China Room. It is one of the most popular rooms among visitors to the White House.

Jacqueline Kennedy No. 2: Of course, everyone is familiar with the large portrait of George Washington that Dolley Madison saved when the White House was burned during the Civil War. It hangs in a very prominent area so that everyone can see it.

Jacqueline Kennedy No. 3: Louisa Adams's harp and Julia Tyler's guitar were both hiding in the attic. I felt it was important to identify each item, so I wrote a book about the artifacts and furnishings titled *The White House: An Historic Guide.* In 1962 I was hostess for a television special, taking the television audience through the restored White House and explaining the history of each room.

Host: Now it is time to decide whose tale is true. We will vote by a show of hands. Is it No. 1? Is it No. 2? Is it No. 3? Now for the moment you have all been waiting for:

Will the real Jacqueline Kennedy step forward?

Answer: No. 3

No. 1 had her dates wrong. The Kennedys moved into the White House in 1961, not 1944.

No. 2 stated that Dolley Madison saved the Washington portrait during the Civil War. She saved the portrait as the British Army was approaching in the War of 1812.

FURTHER READING

Dareff, Hal. *Jacqueline Kennedy: A Portrait in Courage.* Parents Magazine Press, 1965.

Gormley, Beatrice. *Jacqueline Kennedy Onassis: Friend of the Arts.* Simon & Schuster, 2002.

FIND SOMEONE WHO . . .

Find a person in your group or class who has done or can do each of the following items. A name can be used only once. The first player who gets a different name for each item is the winner.

FIND SOMEONE WHO

1. Knows a person who holds an elected office. _____

2. Can name the present first lady. _____

3. Can name the three branches of government. _____

4. Knows how old one has to be to vote. _____

5. Knows the youngest age one can be and become president of the United States.

_____

6. Knows the street address of the White House. _____

7. Can name two political parties. _____

8. Can name the wives of the last three presidents of the United States.

_____

9. Can name a first lady whose children lived in the White House.

_____

10. Can name a first lady who didn't like being the first lady.

_____

Part Four

Twentieth and
Twenty-first Centuries

Claudia Taylor (Lady Bird) Johnson (1912–2007)

First Lady Who Made America Beautiful

Reading Parts: Host, Lady Bird Johnson No. 1, Lady Bird Johnson No. 2, Lady Bird Johnson No. 3

Host: [facing audience] Welcome to "Whose Tale Is True?" Each of our three guests claims to be the lady who made America beautiful, Lady Bird Johnson. Only one, however, is telling the complete truth. It is up to you to decide which one is the real Lady Bird Johnson. Now let's meet our guests. [facing readers] Welcome. When you were a little girl, did you ever dream you would one day be the first lady of America?

Lady Bird Johnson No. 1: I was born in 1912 near the little town of Karnack, Texas. My mother died when I was five years old, so I spent much of my childhood playing in the woods, watching small woodland animals and planting wildflowers where none grew. I'm not sure I even knew what a first lady was supposed to do.

Lady Bird Johnson No. 2: I was born in 1912 in a country mansion. My father was a prosperous storekeeper. I lost my mother at an early age, and the aunt who came to take care of me didn't mind what I did all day as long as I showed up for meals. I spent a lot of time learning about business in my father's store. I even showed my father how to keep all of his records on the computer.

Lady Bird Johnson No. 3: I lost my mother at an early age and was reared by my father, an aunt, and the household servants. I went to a small rural school. When it was time for me to attend high school, which was some distance away, my father taught me to drive, and I drove myself to and from school. I was 13 and had no dreams at all of being the first lady.

Host: We all know that your name is linked to keeping America beautiful. How did that come about?

Lady Bird Johnson No. 1: I have always had a love of nature, and when my husband, Mr. Johnson, became the president, I used the spotlight to plead with people to keep their roads clean and to beautify America by planting wildflowers. With the help of friends I planted thousands of tulips and daffodils in Washington for visitors to enjoy.

From *Whose Tale Is True?: Readers Theatre to Introduce and Research 49 Amazing American Women* by Nancy Polette. Westport, CT: Teacher Ideas Press. Copyright © 2008.

Lady Bird Johnson No. 2: I had always been concerned about our nation's highways, which were littered with trash and ugly billboards. I traveled thousands of miles throughout the country, telling the people it was up to all of us to keep our country clean and beautiful.

Lady Bird Johnson No. 3: Because there were no really good schools in the tiny Texas town where I lived as a child, my father sent me away to a finishing school in Switzerland. He expected me to learn all the social graces. He knew this would help my dream of one day being the first lady come true.

Host: Do you feel your efforts in beautifying America paid off?

Lady Bird Johnson No. 1: Yes, I do. Many laws have been passed to keep highways clutter free. The most important one was the Highway Beautification Act of 1965. I received the Native Plant Conservation Initiative Lifetime Achievement Award for my efforts.

Lady Bird Johnson No. 2: In addition to traveling the country, I served as a member of the National Parks Advisory Board and on other projects to create scenic bike trails with flowering trees.

Lady Bird Johnson No. 3: In 1972 I gave money and land to establish the National Wildlife Research Center, dedicated to restoring native plants to their natural settings. It was a dream come true when the center outgrew its first home and moved to a new facility in 1995.

Host: Now it is time to decide whose tale is true. We will vote by a show of hands. Is it No. 1 Is it No. 2? Is it No. 3? Now for the moment you have all been waiting for:

Will the real Lady Bird Johnson step forward?

Answer: No. 1

No. 2 mentioned using a computer. There were none in local stores when she was growing up.

No. 3 contradicted herself. First she said she had no dreams of being the first lady, then she said she did dream of being the first lady.

FURTHER READING

Appett, Kathi. *Miss Lady Bird's Wildflowers.* HarperCollins, 2005.

Horwitz, Margot. *Claudia Taylor (Lady Bird) Johnson.* Children's Press, 1998.

From *Whose Tale Is True?: Readers Theatre to Introduce and Research 49 Amazing American Women* by Nancy Polette. Westport, CT: Teacher Ideas Press. Copyright © 2008.

PLANT LIFE

Working with a partner, mark these statements yes or no. Then read the booktalk to support or deny your guesses.

———— 1. When you pinch Touch-Me-Not seed pods, the seeds pop out.

———— 2. Indians used Mullen leaves to keep their feet warm.

———— 3. People in Ireland think dandelion juice cures warts.

Booktalk

A Child's Book of Wildflowers, by M. A. Kelly. Illustrated by Joyce Powzyk. Four Winds Press, 1993.

It is as near as your backyard, as close as the empty lot at the end of the block or the meadow out behind the barn. It is as easy as blowing dandelion puffs on a summer day, as lively as the seeds that pop out of Touch-Me-Nots, as fascinating as the face of a sunflower. Welcome to the world of wildflowers, where the Irish found a cure for warts in dandelion juice and Indians survived the cold with Mullen leaves. From Bouncing Bet to goldenrod to evening primrose, here is a guide to the myth and history surrounding these plants.

Activity

Take a guess: How were these plants used long ago?

Match the plant with a use people have found for it.

Plant		Use
_____	milkweed	1. soap
_____	pokeweed	2. glue
_____	mint	3. bath
_____	Bouncing Bet	4. salad
_____	chicory	5. paint

These and many other uses for wildflowers can be found in this book and other books about wildflowers.

⚷ **Answer Key:** milkweed-2; pokeweed-5; mint-3; Bouncing Bet-1; chicory-4

From *Whose Tale Is True?: Readers Theatre to Introduce and Research 49 Amazing American Women* by Nancy Polette. Westport, CT: Teacher Ideas Press. Copyright © 2008.

Shirley Temple Black (1928–   )

From Child Star to Ambassador

Reading Parts: Host, Shirley Temple No. 1, Shirley Temple No. 2, Shirley Temple No. 3

Host: [facing audience] Welcome to "Whose Tale Is True?" Each of our three guests claims to be former child superstar Shirley Temple. Only one, however, is telling the complete truth. It is up to you to decide which one is the real Shirley Temple. Now let's meet our guests. [facing readers] Welcome. Before you were 12 years old, you had starred in more than 40 motion pictures. How did you get started in show business?

Shirley Temple No. 1: My mother said that my first words were words to a song, and she knew from the first that I would be a child star. She took me to lost of auditions and sent videotapes to every producer she could find.

Shirley Temple No. 2: When I was five years old my mother got me a job in a movie studio that did parodies of famous stars. The short movies were called "Baby Burlesque." The studio went out of business, but a producer at Fox studios saw one of the films and signed me to a contract. No one paid much attention to the first five pictures I did for Fox.

Shirley Temple No. 3: In 1934, when I was six, I starred in *Stand Up and Cheer*. The picture was a national sensation. The nation was in the midst of the Great Depression, and my picture helped them forget the hard times for a while. I made 40 films before I was 12 years old.

Host: With that impressive number of films, it's too bad that child stars don't receive an Academy Award.

Shirley Temple No. 1: Awards don't mean much to a six-year-old. I did like all the attention and had fun singing and dancing in the movies. The recording I did of "On the Good Ship Lollipop" sold a half a million copies. I continued to make seven to eight films a year until I became a teenager. A made a few films after that, but they weren't the hits the earlier films had been.

From *Whose Tale Is True?: Readers Theatre to Introduce and Research 49 Amazing American Women* by Nancy Polette. Westport, CT: Teacher Ideas Press. Copyright © 2008.

Shirley Temple No. 2: I was six years old when Fox Studio signed me to a contract. The first film I did for them, *Stand Up and Cheer*, was a big hit. In the nest six years I did six to eight films a year. The last film I did for Fox was *The Bluebird* in 1940.

Shirley Temple No. 3: Once I reached my late teens, I knew it was time to retire from show business. I did some radio and TV work in the 1950s but never made another feature film. I married Charles Black, who supported my wish to lead a life of public service.

Host: What about your adult life makes you most proud?

Shirley Temple No. 1: It's hard to say. Each experience was rewarding in its own way. I was U.S. Representative to the United Nations in 1969. Working with other nations for world peace was a very important job, and I took it very seriously.

Shirley Temple No. 2: President Gerald Ford appointed me ambassador to the Republic of Ghana. Later I became the first woman White House chief of protocol, and under President Ronald Reagan I was a foreign affairs officer with the State Department. Whatever job I was asked to do, I tried to give my best.

Shirley Temple No. 3: I was fortunate to be able to move from the movie stage to the international stage and to serve my country in many ways, as a UN representative, a foreign affairs officer, chief of protocol at the White House, and ambassador to Ghana and Czechoslovakia. It has been a most exciting and rewarding life, and I hope to continue to serve my country in whatever capacity I can.

Host: Now it is time to decide whose tale is true. We will vote by a show of hands. Is it No. 1? Is it No. 2? Is it No. 3? Now for the moment you have all been waiting for:

Will the real Shirley Temple Black step forward?

Answer: No. 3

No. 1 mentioned videotapes, which were not in existence in the 1930s.

No. 2 contradicted herself. First she said no one paid attention to her first five pictures at Fox, then she said her first picture at Fox was a big hit.

FURTHER READING

Bankston, John. *Shirley Temple.* Mitchell Lane, 2004.

Haskins, Jane. *Shirley Temple Black: Actress to Ambassador.* Viking, 1988.

From *Whose Tale Is True?: Readers Theatre to Introduce and Research 49 Amazing American Women* by Nancy Polette. Westport, CT: Teacher Ideas Press. Copyright © 2008.

CHILD STARS OF THE 1930s AND 1940s

A Quiz for Senior Citizens

These children were very popular movie stars 60 to 70 years ago. Many of their films are available today and are fun to watch on television channels that feature old movies. Many public libraries have films made by these children that are available for checkout .

Ask senior citizens you know if they remember seeing any of these children in movies when they were young. In the 1930s and 1940s movie admission was about 25 cents.

How many child stars and their films can seniors match?

1. ____ Elizabeth Taylor	A. *Treasure Island*
2. ____ Jane Withers	B. *How Green Was My Valley*
3. ____ Virginia Weidler	C. *Little Miss Marker*
4. ____ Margaret O'Brien	D. *Boys' Town*
5. ____ Shirley Temple	E. *National Velvet*
6. ____ Deanna Durbin	F. *Pack Up Your Troubles*
7. ____ Jackie Cooper	G. *The Philadelphia Story*
8. ____ Mickey Rooney	H. *David Copperfield*
9. ____ Roddy McDowall	I. *The Canterville Ghost*
10. ____ Freddie Bartholomew	J. *Three Smart Girls*

Read about one of these child stars in the encyclopedia or on the Internet. Do you think it would be fun to be a child movie star? Give reasons why and why not.

WHY?	WHY NOT?

Answer Key: 1-E; 2-F; 3-G; 4-I; 5-C; 6-J; 7-A; 8-D; 9-B; 10-H

Sally Ride (1951–   )

First American Female Astronaut

Reading Parts: Host, Sally Ride No. 1, Sally Ride No. 2, Sally Ride No. 3

Host: [facing audience] Welcome to "Whose Tale Is True?" Each of our three guests claims to be the first female astronaut. Only one, however, is telling the complete truth. It is up to you to decide which one is the real Sally Ride. Now let's meet our guests. [facing readers] Welcome. Did you dream of traveling through space when you were a child?

Sally Ride No. 1: Not at all. I was born in 1951 and was six years old when the Russians sent a dog into space in 1957 and nine years old in 1961 when the Americans launched the first *Mercury* spacecraft. Most Americans, including myself, knew very little about space travel at that time.

Sally Ride No. 2: I was born in 1951 and grew up in Encino, California. My first love was tennis, and I worked hard at becoming a champion. When I was in high school I achieved national ranking and planned to spend my next years as a professional player.

Sally Ride No. 3: Tennis, not space travel, was my first love as a child. I was pretty good at it and as a teen earned extra money as a tennis instructor. I worked hard at the game but finally realized I didn't quite have what it took to be a professional. I knew I would have to look elsewhere for a career.

Host: How did your education prepare you to be an astronaut?

Sally Ride No. 1: At first I wasn't sure what I wanted to study, so I earned two undergraduate degrees at Stanford University, one in physics and one in English.

Sally Ride No. 2: I earned a PhD in physics there in 1977 and then saw a newspaper ad for the astronaut program. I answered the ad along with 8,000 other people. I was fortunate to be one of the 35 people accepted.

Sally Ride No. 3: When I saw a newspaper ad asking for applicants to the astronaut program, I thought that my college degrees might help me qualify. They did, and although a Russian was the first woman in space, in 1963, I became the first American woman to travel into space.

Host: Do you feel your training really prepared you for your first space mission?

Sally Ride No. 1: The training was intensive. I entered the program in 1978 and was one of the five-member crew aboard the shuttle *Challenger* on a six-day mission in 1983. One of our jobs was to deploy satellites for Canada and to retrieve a test satellite. The next year I flew an eight-day mission.

Sally Ride No. 2: Many scientific experiments are performed in space, and my doctorate in biology made me an ideal person to perform such experiments. After being accepted in the program, one of the first things I had to do was to obtain a pilot's license. We all had hours and hours of instruction on spacecraft as well as learning how to stay alive in wild places.

Sally Ride No. 3: The training did prepare me for the missions I flew. I was scheduled for a third mission in 1986 but was asked instead to serve on the Presidential Commission on Space Shuttle Accidents. In 1989 I left the program to become director of the California Space Institute and professor of physics at the University of California.

Host: Now it is time to decide whose tale is true. We will vote by a show of hands. Is it No. 1? Is it No. 2? Is it No. 3? Now for the moment you have all been waiting for:

Will the real Sally Ride step forward?

Answer: No. 3

No. 1 said she was nine years old in 1961, but she had to be 10.

No. 2 first stated her PhD was in physics, then said it was in biology.

FURTHER READING

Gomez, Rebecca. *Sally Ride.* Abdo Publishing, 2003.

Wyborny, Sheila. *Astronauts.* Lucent Books, 2001.

From *Whose Tale Is True?: Readers Theatre to Introduce and Research 49 Amazing American Women* by Nancy Polette. Westport, CT: Teacher Ideas Press. Copyright © 2008.

REPORTING ON SALLY RIDE

Complete this pattern report by adding appropriate information about Sally Ride.

In 1951 the United States was at war with Korea.

In 1951 Sally Ride _____.

In 1961 the United States launched its first manned space flight.

In 1961 Sally Ride celebrated her _____ birthday.

In 1965 the United States launched the *Gemini* flight with two astronauts.

In 1965 Sally ride's greatest interest was _____.

In 1969 U.S. astronauts landed on the moon.

In 1969 Sally ride was a _____-year-old college student.

Between 1975 and 1978 the Soviet Union made its first attempts to launch a space station.

From 1975 to 1978 Sally Ride received _____

_____

In 1978 NASA advertised for prospective astronauts.

In 1978 Sally Ride _____

In 1983 Sally Ride became _____

_____

Answer Key: 1951-was born; 1961-tenth; 1965-tennis; 1969-18; 1975–1978-a BS & a PhD; 1978-was accepted into astronaut program; 1983-the first American woman in space

From *Whose Tale Is True?: Readers Theatre to Introduce and Research 49 Amazing American Women* by Nancy Polette. Westport, CT: Teacher Ideas Press. Copyright © 2008.

Madeleine Albright (1937–   )

First Woman Secretary of State

Reading Parts: Host, Madeleine Albright No. 1, Madeleine Albright No. 2, Madeleine Albright No. 3

Host: [facing audience] Welcome to "Whose Tale Is True?" Each of our three guests claims to be Madeleine Albright, the first woman Secretary of State. Only one, however, is telling the complete truth. It is up to you to decide which one is the real Madeleine Albright. Now let's meet our guests. [facing readers] Welcome, does it seem somewhat amazing to you, as it does to us, that a little girl born in Czechoslovakia would 59 years later become the highest ranking woman in the history of the U.S. government?

Madeleine Albright No. 1: It is true that I was born in Prague, Czechoslovakia, in 1937. My father was a Czech diplomat, and my family fled Czechoslovakia and went to England when I was two years old to escape the Nazis, who invaded our country.

Madeleine Albright No. 2: My family had to escape from Czechoslovakia not only once but twice. We returned to our home country at the end of World War II in 1941 but had to flee from the Communists, who took over the country in 1948.

Madeleine Albright No. 3: When my family left Czechoslovakia in 1948 we came to the United States. I completed my education here, receiving a BA from Wellesley College and a PhD from Columbia University. I have dedicated my life to international affairs and read and speak Czech, French, Russian, and Polish.

Host: We understand that you served as the U.S. permanent representative to the United Nations and on President William Clinton's National Security Council. How did this happen?

Madeleine Albright No. 1: During the Republican years of Presidents Ronald Reagan and George H. W. Bush I worked for many nonprofit organizations, including the Center for National Policy and Professor of International Affairs and as director of the Women in Foreign Service Program at Georgetown University. My work caught the eye of President Clinton, who appointed me as U.S. Representative to the United Nations.

Madeleine Albright No. 2: During the 1980s and early 1990s many important political figures were guests in my home. We had long discussions on international affairs, and I gained a reputation for being very knowledgeable in that area as well as a tough defender of U.S. foreign policy. When a Democratic president was elected in 1992, my name came up as a candidate for UN representative and I was selected by President Clinton.

Madeleine Albright No. 3: My knowledge of foreign relations was well known to the leaders in the Democratic party. When Bill Clinton was elected president, my name was immediately put forward as UN representative. The fact that I did not speak Russian was not considered a detriment.

Host: How do you rank yourself as one of the many secretaries of state the United States has had?

Madeleine Albright No. 1: I did not find being a woman was a handicap in dealing with heads of other nations. Once they discovered I knew what I was talking about, they were willing to listen to the policies of the United States and found me to be a tough adversary when necessary.

Madeleine Albright No. 2: My biggest job was to bring about a bipartisan approach to U.S. foreign policy on the part of the U.S. Congress. I believe I handled it well.

Madeleine Albright No. 3: As a the first woman secretary of state I had to be more knowledgeable and perhaps tougher in dealing with other nations than those who went before me. I am proud of the job I did.

Host: Now it is time to decide whose tale is true. We will vote by a show of hands. Is it No. 1? Is it No. 2? Is it No. 3? Now for the moment you have all been waiting for:

Will the real Madeleine Albright step forward?

> **Answer: No. 1**
>
> No. 2 said World War II ended in 1941. It ended in 1945.
>
> No. 3 contradicted herself. In one response she said she could speak and read Russian. Later she said she could not speak Russian.

FURTHER READING

Byman, Jeremy. *Madame Secretary: The Story of Madeleine Albright.* Morgan-Reynolds, 1998.

Freedman, Suzanne. *Madeleine Albright: She Speaks for America.* Franklin Watts, 1998.

FIND OUT ABOUT IMMIGRANTS

Madeleine Albright came to the United States as an immigrant. How can a person born in another country become a citizen of the United States? Check the almanac for the basic requirements and complete the fact/opinion chart.

STATEMENT	FACT	OPINION	PROOF*
The minimum age to apply for citizenship is 18.			
Children born in the United States of immigrant parents are not U.S. citizens.			
An applicant must have been a resident of the United States for five or more years.			
It is not necessary for an applicant to read, write, and speak English.			
Applicants must demonstrate a knowledge of the Constitution and of U.S. history.			
Applicants must swear an oath of allegiance to the United States.			

*For proof write the almanac page number on which the information appears.

From *Whose Tale Is True?: Readers Theatre to Introduce and Research 49 Amazing American Women* by Nancy Polette. Westport, CT: Teacher Ideas Press. Copyright © 2008.

Carol Burnett (1933–   )

She Brought Smiles

Reading Parts: Host, Carol Burnett No. 1, Carol Burnett No. 2, Carol Burnett No. 3

Host: [facing audience] Welcome to "Whose Tale Is True?" Each of our three guests claims to be Carol Burnett, star of stage and television. Only one, however, is telling the complete truth. It is up to you to decide which one is the real Carol Burnett. Now let's meet our guests. [facing readers] Welcome. It seems that given your background, your rise to fame on the stage and in television was truly amazing. Tell us how this came about.

Carol Burnett No. 1: I was born in San Antonio, Texas, in 1933 to parents who were both alcoholics. We had very little money, and my parents were not able to take care of me, so I was sent to an orphanage.

Carol Burnett No. 2: Don't believe a word she says. She just wants sympathy. Yes, we were poor and my parents were alcoholics, but I was sent to live with my grandmother, who gave me all the love and care any child could want.

Carol Burnett No. 3: My grandmother ran a boarding house in Hollywood. It was a house that had been owned previously by Harry James and Betty Grable. I liked performing for the boarders. I even fooled them into thinking I was my own twin.

Host: How did you end up with parts on Broadway and in television?

Carol Burnett No. 1: My grandmother, who raised me, made sure I got an education. I graduated from Hollywood High School and attended the University of California. From acting classes there I got bit parts on TV.

Carol Burnett No. 2: After my first TV appearance on the *Paul Winchell Show* in 1955, I became a regular on the game show *Pantomime Quiz*. That led to a part on Broadway in *Once Upon a Mattress* and a job as a regular on the *Garry Moore Show* in 1959.

Carol Burnett No. 3: My three years on the *Garry Moore Show* from 1959 until 1965 rocketed me to stardom. My crazy antics and funny sketches week after week started a love affair between me and the TV viewing audience. I won an Emmy in 1962 for outstanding performance in a variety series.

Host: Are there any people you feel were especially helpful to you in your career?

Carol Burnett No. 1: Almost too many to name. My grandmother, of course, encouraged me as a performer. My mother said I should write because I wasn't pretty enough to perform on the stage. My husband, Joe Hamilton, always encouraged me to do my best and to take risks in trying new things as a performer.

Carol Burnett No. 2: Garry Moore gave me my first real break as a performer by having me on his show. My own variety show in 1967 would never have lasted 11 years without the marvelous Harvey Korman, Tim Conway, Lyle Waggoner, and Vicki Lawrence.

Carol Burnett No. 3: Lucille Ball was a good friend and mentor and gave me many helpful tips as a performer. We were the best of friends.

Host: Now it is time to decide whose tale is true. We will vote by a show of hands. Is it No. 1? Is it No. 2? Is it No. 3? Now for the moment you have all been waiting for:

Will the real Carol Burnett step forward?

Answer: No. 2

No. 1 contradicted herself about where she was raised.

No. 3 mixed up her dates; 1959–1965 is not three years.

FURTHER READING

Howe, James. *Carol Burnett: The Sound of Laughter*. Viking, 1987.

Paige, David. *Carol Burnett*. Creative Education, 1977.

A CAROL BURNETT BIO-POEM

Tell about Carol Burnett using the bio-poem model below.

I AM _____

I WONDER _____

I HEAR _____

I SEE _____

I WANT _____

I PRETEND _____

I TOUCH _____

I CRY _____

I SAY _____

I TRY _____

I GIVE _____

I AM _____

Oprah Winfrey (1954–   )

Actress and Television Host

Reading Parts: Host, Oprah Winfrey No. 1, Oprah Winfrey No. 2, Oprah Winfrey No. 3

Host: [facing audience] Welcome to "Whose Tale Is True?" Each of our three guests claims to be Oprah Winfrey, actress and television host. Only one, however, is telling the complete truth. It is up to you to decide which one is the real Oprah Winfrey. Now let's meet our guests. [facing readers] Welcome. Is it true that you have always had a talent for talk?

Oprah Winfrey No. 1: As a very young child I lived with my grandmother, who was very religious. She taught me to read at the age of three and I gave short Bible talks at church on special days.

Oprah Winfrey No. 2: I gave my first speeches in church before I was old enough to go to school. I lived with my grandmother, who was loving but strict, until I was six years old, then I went to Milwaukee to live with my mother, and later, as a teen, I was sent to Nashville to live with my father. I never saw my grandmother again.

Oprah Winfrey No. 3: When I was 12 I was paid $500 for a speech I gave in church. I was living with my grandmother at the time, and she was very proud of me. I was sent to high school and college in Mississippi and did well.

Host: How did you manage to connect with a television station?

Oprah Winfrey No. 1: When I went to Milwaukee to live with my mother, life in the ghetto was rough and I had a tough time there. I rebelled and tried running away, so my mother gave up on me and sent me to live with my father in Nashville. He insisted I stay in school and do well. I did so well that I got a part time job with a Nashville TV station when I was still in high school.

Oprah Winfrey No. 2: My mother and I didn't get along, and I was pretty hard to handle as a teenager, so my mother sent me back to live on the Mississippi farm with my grandmother. A television producer heard me speak in church and hired me part time at his TV station in Mississippi.

Oprah Winfrey No. 3: When I was six I left my grandmother and went to live with my mother. By the time I was 13 I was a rebellious runaway, so my mother sent me to live with my father in Nashville. He put me on the straight and narrow, and I did so well in school that I got a college scholarship and a job with radio station WVOL.

Host: Your rise to fame was spectacular, wasn't it?

Oprah Winfrey No. 1: It was not overnight stardom, if that's what you mean. When I graduated from college I got a job as a co-anchor on an ABC television station in Baltimore, Maryland. After nine years I was co-host of a morning show called *People Are Talking*.

Oprah Winfrey No. 2: I did much better talking with guests on the morning show than I did reporting the news. In fact, I did so well that in 1984 I got my own show in Chicago called *A.M. Chicago*. After one year the show was renamed the *Oprah Winfrey Show*.

Oprah Winfrey No. 3: It took 11 years from the time I first appeared on television until I had my own show. They were years of hard work and led not only to the *Oprah Winfrey Show*, but to movie roles as well.

Host: Now it is time to decide whose tale is true. We will vote by a show of hands. Is it No. 1? Is it No. 2? Is it No. 3? Now for the moment you have all been waiting for:

Will the real Oprah Winfrey step forward?

Answer: No. 1

No. 2 contradicted herself; she did not return to her grandmother as a teen.

No. 3 contradicted herself; she did not live with her grandmother at age 12.

FURTHER READING

Friedrich, Belinda. *Oprah Winfrey*. Chelsea House, 2001.

Mara, Will. *Oprah Winfrey*. Children's Press, 2005.

FIRSTS FOR WOMEN

Oprah Winfrey became Nashville's first black female co-anchor on the evening television news.

Match these women with the accomplishment that made them first in their fields.

FIRST WOMAN

1. _____ To be pictured on a U.S. coin   A. Elizabeth Blackwell

2. _____ To run for president of the United States   B. Eileen Collins

3. _____ To be elected a state governor   C. Sandra Day O'Connor

4. _____ To swim the English Channel   D. Madeleine Albright

5. _____ To fly across the Atlantic   E. Amelia Earhart

6. _____ To be a female jockey   F. Susan B. Anthony

7. _____ To be appointed to the Supreme Court   G. Nellie Ross

8. _____ To command a space shuttle   H. Victoria Woodhull

9. _____ To become secretary of state of the United States   I. Gertrude Ederle

10. _____ To receive a medical degree   J. Diane Crump

Answer Key: 1-F; 2-H; 3-G; 4-I; 5-E; 6-J; 7-C; 8-B; 9-D; 10-A

Sandra Day O'Connor (1930–   )

First Woman Supreme Court Justice

Reading Parts: Host, Sandra Day O'Connor No. 1, Sandra Day O'Connor No. 2, Sandra Day O'Connor No. 3

Host: [facing audience] Welcome to "Whose Tale Is True?" Each of our three guests claims to be former Supreme Court Justice, Sandra Day O'Connor. Only one, however, is telling the complete truth. It is up to you to decide which one is the real Sandra Day O'Connor. Now let's meet our guests. [facing readers] Welcome. Tell us how you managed to go from life on a cattle ranch to becoming the first woman Supreme Court justice.

Sandra Day O'Connor No. 1: I was born in 1930 in El Paso, Texas, where my family had a 198,000-acre cattle ranch. My early days were spent riding and roping steers. I gave little thought then to how I would spend my life.

Sandra Day O'Connor No. 2: I was born in 1930 and raised on a cattle ranch until I reached age six. There were few good schools near the ranch, so my parents sent me to live with my grandmother and go to school in El Paso, Texas.

Sandra Day O'Connor No. 3: I was born in El Paso, Texas, in 1930 and spent my early years on my parents' cattle ranch in Duncan, Arizona. When I reached school age I went to live with my grandmother in El Paso, Texas, where I completed grade school and high school. I then went on to Stanford University for both my BS and law degrees.

Host: What got you interested in the law?

Sandra Day O'Connor No. 1: In 1940 I graduated from Stanford University with a degree in economics. Becoming a lawyer seemed the next logical step.

Sandra Day O'Connor No. 2: After high school I attended Stanford University, where I eventually got a law degree. I was third in a class of 102 but no law firm would hire me after graduation be-

From *Whose Tale Is True?: Readers Theatre to Introduce and Research 49 Amazing American Women* by Nancy Polette. Westport, CT: Teacher Ideas Press. Copyright © 2008.

Sandra Day O'Connor No. 3: cause I was a woman. I eventually got a job as assistant attorney general for Arizona.

Sandra Day O'Connor No. 3: There were few women lawyers in 1952 when I left our Texas cattle ranch and eventually graduated from law school. I couldn't find a job because law firms were closed to women applicants. In the meantime I married John O'Connor and went to Germany with him, where I worked as a civil attorney for the U.S. army.

Host: Tell us about your rise to the Supreme Court.

Sandra Day O'Connor No. 1: After serving as assistant attorney general in Arizona for four years, I was appointed to fill a seat in the Arizona Senate. In 1974 I won election as a trial judge and my rulings were considered to be thoughtful and fair. My record caught the attention of people in Washington.

Sandra Day O'Connor No. 2: From my position as a trial judge I was appointed to the Arizona Court of Appeals in 1979. My rulings made it obvious that I saw my job as interpreting the law and not as a legislator. This caught the attention of President Ronald Reagan, who appointed me to the Supreme Court.

Sandra Day O'Connor No. 3: It seems that one door opens another. I went from being assistant attorney general to the Arizona Senate, to being a trial judge, to the Arizona Court of Appeals, and finally to the Supreme Court. I tried to give my best to each and every job.

Host: Now it is time to decide whose tale is true. We will vote by a show of hands. Is it No. 1? Is it No. 2? Is it No. 3? Now for the moment you have all been waiting for:

Will the real Sandra Day O'Connor step forward?

Answer: No. 2

No. 1 said she was born in 1930 and graduated from the university in 1940.

No. 3 said the ranch where she was raised was in Texas, then said it was in Arizona.

FURTHER READING

Greene, Carol. *Sandra Day O'Connor: First Woman on the Supreme Court*. Children's Press, 1982.

McElroy, Lisa. *Sandra Day O'Connor: Supreme Court Justice*. Millbrook Press, 2003.

HAVE A CONTEST!

Give one card to teams of two or three. Each card names a woman who was a leader in some field. The team who completes the information on the card first is the winner.

Vaira Freiburga	Margaret Chase Smith	Margaret Thatcher
What?	What?	What?
When?	When?	When?
Where?	Where?	Where?

Indira Gandhi	Eileen Collins	Shirley Chisholm
What?	What?	What?
When?	When?	When?
Where?	Where?	Where?

Dr. Mae C. Jemison (1956–   )

First Black Woman Astronaut

Reading Parts: Host, Mae Jemison No. 1, Mae Jemison No. 2, Mae Jemison No. 3

Host: [facing audience] Welcome to "Whose Tale Is True?" Each of our three guests claims to be astronaut Dr. Mae C. Jemison. Only one, however, is telling the complete truth. It is up to you to decide which one is the real Dr. Jemison. Now let's meet our guests. [facing readers] Welcome. You seem to be a woman of many interests. Who or what aroused your interest in science and space travel?

Mae Jemison No. 1: I was born in 1956 in Decatur, Alabama, but grew up and attended high school in Chicago. My mother was a school teacher and impressed on all of her children the importance of an education.

Mae Jemison No. 2: It was while I was growing up in Chicago that an uncle introduced me to the world of science. I was fascinated by all things scientific, and after high school I enrolled at Stanford University, where I earned degrees in chemical engineering and African American studies.

Mae Jemison No. 3: I was born in Decatur, Alabama, in 1956 but grew up in Chicago. I was 10 years old when Alan Shepard made the first space flight in 1961, and I vowed right then and there that one day I would travel in space.

Host: Did you feel that your college degree in chemical engineering would qualify you for space travel?

Mae Jemison No. 1: That degree was only the beginning. My mother was a medical doctor, and she urged me to study medicine. I received a doctor of medicine degree in 1981. I worked as a doctor for the Peace Corps in Africa for two years and then returned to practice medicine in the United States. It was then that I applied for admission to the astronaut program.

Mae Jemison No. 2: After earning a medical degree and working in Africa for the Peace Corps, I applied for admission to the astronaut program in 1986 but was turned down. I applied again a year later and was accepted. That year there were 2,000 applicants, but only 15 of us were chosen.

Mae Jemison No. 3: I was working as a family doctor in Los Angeles when NASA accepted me for training in the astronaut program. My task would be to conduct scientific experiments in space. I was thrilled to be given such an important responsibility.

Host: Tell us about the space flight that you made.

Mae Jemison No. 1: In September 1992 I was a member of the crew of the space shuttle *Endeavor*. It was a week-long mission, and my experiments in the life sciences were carried out without a hitch.

Mae Jemison No. 2: When our space shuttle, *Endeavor*, entered space I could look back at Earth and pretend I could see Chicago, the place where my dream to become an astronaut began. It was a humbling sight.

Mae Jemison No. 3: I made only the one space flight and worked for NASA for some time after that. Upon leaving NASA I formed the Jemison Group, Inc. to encourage African Americans to pursue careers in science and engineering and to improve health in Africa.

Host: Now it is time to decide whose tale is true. We will vote by a show of hands. Is it No. 1? Is it No. 2? Is it No. 3? Now for the moment you have all been waiting for:

Will the real Dr. Mae C. Jemison step forward?

Answer: No. 2

No. 1 first said her mother was a school teacher, then said she was a medical doctor.

No. 3 could not have been 10 years old in 1961 when she was born in 1956.

FURTHER READING

Polette, Nancy. *Mae Jemison*. Children's Press, 2003.

Sakurai, Gail. *Mae Jemison, Space Scientist*. Children's Press, 1995.

FIND THESE FIRSTS IN SPACE

1. The name of the first pilot to break the sound barrier (in 1947).

_____

2. The name of the first craft ever launched into space, sent by the Russians in 1957.

_____

3. The name of the first human being to go into space (April 12, 1961).

_____

4. The name of the first American to travel into space (May 5, 1961).

_____

5. The name of the first American to walk in space (June 3, 1965).

_____

6. The name of the first person to walk on the moon (July 16, 1969).

_____

7. The first man-made object to escape the solar system (March 3, 1972).

_____

8. The name of America's space station, launched on May 14, 1974.

_____

9. The first American woman to orbit the earth (June 18, 1983).

_____

Answer Key: 1-Chuck Yeager; 2-*Sputnik*; 3-Yuri Gagarin; 4-Alan Shepard; 5-Ed White; 6-Neil Armstrong; 7-*Pioneer 10*; 8-*Skylab*; 9-Sally Ride

From *Whose Tale Is True?: Readers Theatre to Introduce and Research 49 Amazing American Women* by Nancy Polette. Westport, CT: Teacher Ideas Press. Copyright © 2008.

Elizabeth Taylor (1932–   )

Star Power

Reading Parts: Host, Elizabeth Taylor No. 1, Elizabeth Taylor No. 2, Elizabeth Taylor No. 3

Host: [facing audience] Welcome to "Whose Tale Is True?" Each of our three guests claims to be Elizabeth Taylor, two-time Academy Award winner. Only one, however, is telling the complete truth. It is up to you to decide which one is the real Elizabeth Taylor. Now let's meet our guests. [facing readers] Welcome. It seems amazing that you have been one of film's greatest stars for more than 60 years. Tell us how this began.

Elizabeth Taylor No. 1: I was born in England of American parents and began ballet lessons when I was three years old. My mother had been an actress. I must have gotten some of my talent from her.

Elizabeth Taylor No. 2: My parents left England at the beginning of World War II, and we made our home in Los Angeles, California. It was there I was spotted by a talent scout, and I made my first movie at age 10 for Universal Studios. It was not exactly a hit. Universal did not renew my contract.

Elizabeth Taylor No. 3: After Universal did not renew my contract I thought I was a has-been at age 10. Then MGM Studios signed me to do *Lassie Come Home* in 1943 with Mickey Rooney and *National Velvet* with Roddy McDowall in 1944. After that it was just one film after another.

Host: How did you manage schooling with all these films?

Elizabeth Taylor No. 1: I attended school on the MGM lot and received a high school diploma in 1950. During my teen years I made movies like *Life with Father* and then moved easily into adult roles in *Raintree County* and *Butterfield 8*, for which I won my first Academy Award in 1960.

Elizabeth Taylor No. 2: My first movie was such a box office hit that talent scouts at MGM saw it and offered me more money that Universal

Elizabeth Taylor No. 3: During the making of *National Velvet* my co-star, Mickey Rooney, and I tried to play hooky from the MGM Studio school, but we got caught every time and were given lots and lots of homework.

Host: What do you think has been the greatest influence on your acting career?

Elizabeth Taylor No. 1: My mother, Sarah Taylor, has always been a strong influence in my life. I have had eight husbands, and from one, Richard Burton, I learned a lot about acting. He was a superb actor.

Elizabeth Taylor No. 2: My strong-willed mother had lots of suggestions about how I should live my life and manage my career. I often listened to her. She would have burst with pride if she had lived to see me made a Dame of the British Empire in 2000. It was quite an honor.

Elizabeth Taylor No. 3: I managed in the 1990s to move from starring roles to those of older women and at the same time started the House of Taylor jewelry business and launched three perfumes, I also created charitable foundations to fight poverty and disease.

Host: Now it is time to decide whose tale is true. We will vote by a show of hands. Is it No. 1? Is it No. 2? Is it No. 3? Now for the moment you have all been waiting for:

Will the real Elizabeth Taylor step forward?

Answer: No. 1

No. 2 contradicted herself. Her first movie was not a box office hit.

No. 3 mixed up her co-stars. Mickey Rooney starred in *National Velvet*, not Roddy McDowall.

FURTHER READING

Taraborrelli, J. Randy. *Elizabeth*. Warner Books, 2006.

Taylor, Elizabeth. *Nibbles and Me*. Simon & Schuster, 2002.

ACADEMY AWARDS

Each year since 1928, the Academy of Motion Picture Arts and Sciences has awarded a gold-plated statuette, nicknamed the Oscar, to the best actor, best actress, and numerous other film categories. Elizabeth Taylor won the Academy Award twice, for her performances in the films *Butterfield 8* and *Who's Afraid of Virginia Woolf*. She was also nominated for three other films in which she starred. In 1963 she was the highest paid movie star, earning as much as $1 million per film.

Use the almanac to answer these questions

1. Ten actresses have won the Academy Award twice. Name five of them.

   _____

   _____

   _____

   _____

2. One actress won the award four times. Who is she?

   _____

   _____

   _____

   _____

3. Check the monthly program guide for old films being shown on AMC (American Movie Classics) or TCM (Turner Classic Movies) for a film starring one of the actresses you listed above. Watch the film. Do you think she deserved the Academy Award? Why or why not?

   _____

   _____

   _____

   _____

Answer Key: 1-Luise Rainer, Bette Davis, Olivia de Havilland, Vivian Leigh, Elizabeth Taylor, Ingrid Bergman, Glenda Jackson, Jane Fonda, Sally Field, Jodie Foster; 2-Katharine Hepburn

From *Whose Tale Is True?: Readers Theatre to Introduce and Research 49 Amazing American Women* by Nancy Polette. Westport, CT: Teacher Ideas Press. Copyright © 2008.

Loretta Lynn (1935–   )

Queen of Country Music

Reading Parts: Host, Loretta Lynn No. 1, Loretta Lynn No. 2, Loretta Lynn No. 3

Host: [facing audience] Welcome to "Whose Tale Is True?" Each of our three guests claims to be Loretta Lynn, country music singer and song writer. Only one, however, is telling the complete truth. It is up to you to decide which one is the real Loretta Lynn. Now let's meet our guests. [facing readers] Welcome. You are nearing fifty years in show business as a country music singer and songwriter. Why do you think your career has lasted so long when many singers just come and go?

Loretta Lynn No. 1: Most of the songs I sing are those I have written. They come from real-life experiences that most women have had. I think women appreciate my voicing their fears and concerns and sometimes their anger.

Loretta Lynn No. 2: I was born in 1935 and grew up in a very poor family. I was married in 1948 at the age of 20, and in the early 1960s, when I started singing in small clubs, I saw performing as a way out of poverty.

Loretta Lynn No. 3: I married at age 13, had four children by the time I was 17, and Mooney, my husband and I, were grandparents when I was 29. Mooney helped me to get my first recording with Zero records in 1960. We drove all over the country to get country music stations to play it.

Host: Was that first record a top hit?

Loretta Lynn No. 1: My first record was "I'm a Honky Tonk Girl." It wasn't a top hit. It only made number 14 on the charts, but it did get me a place in the Grand Ole Opry. Within the next few years I became the number one female recording artist in country music.

Loretta Lynn No. 2: I made the mistake of giving publishing rights to my songs to a record company. When I left the company I did not get the rights back, so I had to stop writing new songs. I hated this because I had a lot more I wanted to say in my music to the women of my day.

Loretta Lynn No. 3: I almost didn't make a first record. My husband, Mooney, thought I should be a full-time mom to our four kids, and he objected to my singing anywhere except at home. I had to make and promote my first record without him knowing anything about it.

Host: Your greatest number of number one hits happened between 1976 and 1981. Is there a reason there were far fewer hits after that?

Loretta Lynn No. 1: Yes. I had moderate success in the 1980s, but Mooney, my husband, had a long illness in the 1990s, and I was needed at home to care for him until his death in 1996. I toured a lot in the 1980s and 1990s, and in 2004 my album *Van Lear Rose* was voted the second best of the year. Not bad for an almost 70-year-old!

Loretta Lynn No. 2: Country music underwent a change in the 1980s, when a more pop-flavored type of music dominated the market. This was a style that did not appeal to me, so I stopped singing and retired from the stage.

Loretta Lynn No. 3: In the early 1980s a film was made of my book, *Coal Miner's Daughter*, which brought me lots of attention, including two NBC prime-time specials. My singing career took off again, and I am still going strong.

Host: Now it is time to decide whose tale is true. We will vote by a show of hands. Is it No. 1? Is it No. 2? Is it No. 3? Now for the moment you have all been waiting for:

Will the real Loretta Lynn step forward?

Answer: No. 1

No. 2 could not have been 20 years old in 1948 if she was born in 1935.

No. 3 contradicted herself. In one response she said her husband, Mooney, helped her to get started on a career in country music. In another response she said he forbade her to sing anywhere except at home.

FURTHER READING

George-Warren, Holly. *Honkey Tonk Heroes and Hillbilly Angels*. Houghton Mifflin, 2006.

Krishef, Robert. *Loretta Lynn*. Lerner Publications, 1976.

THE ANNUAL MUSIC AWARD

Loretta Lynn achieved fame both as a singer and as a composer of music. Here are six other outstanding women performers in the country music field.

Kitty Wells	Dolly Parton	Tammy Wynette
Patsy Cline	Skeeter Davis	Jean Shepard

Choose one to research. What was it that led the woman to achieve star status? Design a music award for that woman. Be sure that the design shows clearly in both words and illustrations the reason for the award.

Barbara Walters (1929–   )

Television Journalist

Reading Parts: Host, Barbara Walters No. 1, Barbara Walters No. 2, Barbara Walters No. 3

Host: [facing audience] Welcome to "Whose Tale Is True?" Each of our three guests claims to be Barbara Walters, television journalist. Only one, however, is telling the complete truth. It is up to you to decide which one is the real Barbara Walters. Now let's meet our guests. [facing readers] Welcome. Your biography states that your first job was in television more than 50 years ago. Is this correct?

Barbara Walters No. 1: Yes. I graduated from Sarah Lawrence College in 1953 and went to work as an assistant to the publicity director at a local television station. I spent several years sharpening my writing and producing skills, then got a job writing for the CBS *Morning Show*. By 1961 I was a writer for the popular CBS *Today Show*.

Barbara Walters No. 2: Since graduation from college in 1953 I have always had some kind of job in television. I have been a writer, producer, interviewer, journalist, co-anchor of a network evening news program, and co-host of a midmorning talk show and have filled many other roles. By 1976 my salary was $1 million a year.

Barbara Walters No. 3: It is true that I have worked for all three major networks. Early in my career I wrote for the CBS *Morning Show* and the NBC *Today Show*, and by 1976 I was co-anchoring the evening news on ABC. My direct and honest approach to the news, along with my clear speaking voice, appealed to viewers.

Host: Is it true that you have interviewed every U.S. president since Richard Nixon?

Barbara Walters No. 1: I interviewed Richard Nixon six years after his resignation in 1974. By that time he was considered to be an elder statesman. Two years before that I launched the *Barbara*

From *Whose Tale Is True?: Readers Theatre to Introduce and Research 49 Amazing American Women* by Nancy Polette. Westport, CT: Teacher Ideas Press. Copyright © 2008.

Walters Special featuring interviews with Jimmy and Rosalynn Carter. I soon became known as an excellent interviewer.

Barbara Walters No. 2: I spent 11 years on the NBC *Today Show* and became known for my probing yet casual interviewing skills. I accompanied First Lady Jacqueline Kennedy on her trip to India, and in 1972 I was chosen to accompany President Nixon on his trip to China. My 1984 interview with Christopher Reeve received the prestigious George Foster Peabody Award.

Barbara Walters No. 3: I have had many different jobs in my long career in television. Most were behind the scenes rather than in front of the cameras, due to my speech. I still have a lisp that I have been unable to correct, and the lisp is irritating to viewers. I have done some on-camera work but prefer to work off camera.

Host: Now it is time to decide whose tale is true. We will vote by a show of hands. Is it No. 1? Is it No. 2? Is it No. 3? Now for the moment you have all been waiting for:

Will the real Barbara Walters step forward?

Answer: No. 2

No. I mentioned the CBS *Today Show*. The *Today Show* was and is on NBC.

No. 3 contradicted herself. In one response she said she had clear speech, then she said her lisp was irritating to viewers.

FURTHER READING

Malone, Mary. *Barbara Walters: TV Superstar*. Enslow Publishers, 1990.

Remstein, Henna. *Barbara Walters*. Chelsea House, 1999.

TAKE THIS TELEVISION QUIZ

How much do you know about television?

Take the quiz. Then check your answers with the answer key.

1. The first coast-to-coast television broadcast happened in

    (A) 1935   (B) 1965   (C) 1951

2. The year color television first appeared was

    (A) 1953   (B) 1963   (C) 1972

3. The average American home has two or more television sets.

    (A) false   (B) true

4. The first moon landing was seen on television in

    (A) 1939   (B) 1949   (C) 1969

5. The average number of hours children and teens view television each week is

    (A) 6   (B) 20   (C) 40

6. U.S. children spend more hours watching TV in a year than they spend in school.

    (A) true   (B) false

7. The country with the largest number of television sets is

    (A) United States (B) India   (C) China

8. What percent of American children have a TV in their bedroom?

    (A) 56%   (B) 10%   (C) 20%

9. The major award given for excellence in television programs is called

    (A) the Oscar   (B) the Emmy   (C) the Golden Globe

10. Girls watch more television each week than boys do.

    (A) true   (B) false

Answer Key: 1-C; 2-A; 3-B; 4-C; 5-B; 6-A; 7-C; 8-A; 9-B; 10-A

From *Whose Tale Is True?: Readers Theatre to Introduce and Research 49 Amazing American Women* by Nancy Polette. Westport, CT: Teacher Ideas Press. Copyright © 2008.

Condoleezza Rice (1954–   )

First Black Woman Secretary of State

Reading Parts: Host, Condoleezza Rice No. 1, Condoleezza Rice No. 2, Condoleezza Rice No. 3

Host: [facing audience] Welcome to "Whose Tale Is True?" Each of our three guests claims to be Condoleezza Rice, the first black woman secretary of state. Only one, however, is telling the complete truth. It is up to you to decide which one is the real Condoleezza Rice. Now let's meet our guests. [facing readers] Welcome. You are a woman of many talents, a seasoned diplomat who has held many government posts, an educator who has received numerous earned and honorary degrees, and an accomplished pianist. What made you choose government service as a career?

Condoleezza Rice No. 1: I grew up in the segregated South and knew many of the indignities of being treated as a second class citizen. My parents felt I would not face discrimination as an adult if I was twice as good at my chosen career as others.

Condoleezza Rice No. 2: Growing up during a time of racial segregation, I was determined to be twice as good as non-minorities. I would prove myself worthy of advancement and had loving parents who gave me every opportunity to excel. I started learning French, music, figure skating, and ballet at the age of three. By age 15 I was practicing every day to become a concert pianist.

Condoleezza Rice No. 3: My father was a minister and my mother was a high school guidance counselor. They knew the value of an education and encouraged me to pursue both undergraduate and graduate degrees. A course in international politics changed my life. I knew this was what I wanted to do.

Host: Tell us how you moved from academics to working in international relations for the government.

Condoleezza Rice No. 1: I was 26 when I received my PhD in political science. A year later I became a professor at Stanford University. I became provost of the university in 1993 and served in that capacity for six years. Many professors did not like it when I opposed affirmative action in promotions. I thought ability should be more important than skin color.

Condoleezza Rice No. 2: When I entered college I gave up the idea of becoming a concert pianist. I studied political science and international relations and earned a doctorate at age 26. After serving as provost of Stanford University I held many government posts, including national security advisor to President George W. Bush.

Condoleezza Rice No. 3: Since neither of my parents had a formal education, they insisted that I do well in school. I fulfilled their dreams by earning a doctorate at Stanford University and by eventually becoming the first African American woman secretary of state.

Host: Was there any one incident in your childhood that led you to become such an overachiever?

Condoleezza Rice No. 1: One of my best friends was killed in the Sixteenth Street Baptist Church bombing in Birmingham in 1963. As a nine-year-old I determined at that terrible moment to lead the fight for affirmative action to give African Americans every possible chance to succeed.

Condoleezza Rice No. 2: I went to a segregated elementary school, was not allowed to use regular dressing rooms in department stores, and was barred from attending the circus or the local amusement park because of the color of my skin. When I was 13 my family moved to Denver, and after high school I attended the University of Denver, where my father was a teacher and an assistant dean.

Condoleezza Rice No. 3: I faced many instances of discrimination, as did most other African Americans. We were often denied hotel rooms or given bad food in restaurants. My father insisted that we had to prove ourselves worthy of advancement and gave me every opportunity to do so.

Host: Now it is time to decide whose tale is true. We will vote by a show of hands. Is it No. 1? Is it No. 2? Is it No. 3? Now for the moment you have all been waiting for:

Will the real Condoleezza Rice step forward?

From *Whose Tale Is True?: Readers Theatre to Introduce and Research 49 Amazing American Women* by Nancy Polette. Westport, CT: Teacher Ideas Press. Copyright © 2008.

Answer: No. 2

No. 1 contradicted herself, first saying she was against and then saying she was for affirmative action.

No. 3 contradicted herself. In one response she said her parents held jobs as a minister and guidance counselor, in another she said they were uneducated.

FURTHER READING

Naden, Corinne J., and Rose Blue. *Condoleezza Rice*. Raintree, 2000.

Wade, Linda R. *Condoleezza Rice*. Mitchell Lane Publishers, 2003.

THE COLORS OF CONDOLEEZZA

Condoleezza Rice firmly believed that a person should be judged by his or her achievements and not by the color of his or her skin.

Many colors could be associated with Condoleezza Rice. Read the play again or locate more information about her. Tell why each of these colors can be used to describe her.

Example:

Purple: The color of royalty should be a cloak that sits on the shoulders of Condoleezza Rice because she has been secretary of state, one of the elite that help to govern our land.

Red _____

_____

_____

Blue _____

_____

_____

Green _____

_____

_____

Yellow _____

_____

_____

Pink _____

_____

_____

CREATE YOUR OWN "WHOSE TALE IS TRUE?"

1. Choose a person you admire.

2. Gather information about that person.

3. Develop three questions the host might ask based on the information you have collected.

4. Develop three answers to each question. Remember that one person must always answer truthfully.

5. Decide which two persons will either contradict themselves in a later speech or include a historical fact that could not possibly be true.

6. Follow the outline to write the script.

From *Whose Tale Is True?: Readers Theatre to Introduce and Research 49 Amazing American Women* by Nancy Polette. Westport, CT: Teacher Ideas Press. Copyright © 2008.

Person's Name _____ (Date[s])

Reading Parts: Host, _____ No. 1,

_____ No. 2, _____ No. 3

Host: Welcome to "Whose Tale Is True?" Each of our three guests claims to be

_____. Only one, however, is telling the complete truth. It is up to you to decide which one is the real _____. Now let's meet our guests. Welcome: (Ask a question)

_____ **No. 1:** _____

_____

_____

_____ **No. 2:** _____

_____

_____

_____ **No. 3:** _____

_____

_____

Host: (Ask a question):

_____

_____

_____

_____ **No. 1:** _____

_____

_____

_____ **No. 2:** _____

_____

_____

_____ **No. 3:** _____

_____

_____

Host: (Ask a question):

_____

_____

_____

_____ **No. 1:** _____

_____

_____

_____ **No. 2:** _____

_____

_____

_____ **No. 3:** _____

_____

_____

Host: Now it is time to decide whose tale is true. We will vote by a show of hands. Is it No. 1? Is it No. 2? Is it No. 3? Now for the moment you have all been waiting for:

Will the real _____ **step forward?**

Answer: Tell which was the real person. _____

Tell why each of the others was not the real person.

_____

_____

Index

About the Author

NANCY POLETTE is an educator with over 30 years' experience. She has authored more than 150 professional books. She lives and works in Missouri, where she is Professor at Lindenwood University.